CHINESE
LOVE SIGNS

CHINESE LOVE SIGNS

Derek Walters

Illustrations by Caroline Rose

HEIAN

By Derek Walters
Illustration by Caroline Rose

Copyright 1994 Derek Walters

Heian International, Inc.
1815 West 205th Street
Torrance, CA 90501

ISBN: 0-89346-840-1

1. Astrology, Chinese 2. Calendar, Chinese 3. Love 4. Signs and Symbols

First American Edition 1997
97 98 99 00 01 9 8 7 6 5 4 3 2 1

Printed in Hong Kong

CONTENTS

'What kind of folk are they who eagerly plunge
into marriage, heedless of the
harmonies of heaven?'

Anon.
from *The Shih Ching*, Book I, IV, 7
(The Classic of Poetry, Chou Dynasty, c. 1000 BC)

INTRODUCTION

Perhaps the biggest decision we ever have to make in our lives is choosing the companion with whom to spend the rest of our days. We cannot choose who we have for parents, nor our brothers and sisters, nor our children. But when it comes to choosing a partner for life, there are options. And if we don't get it right, what problems there will be!

For countless generations, Chinese people have known that a pretty face and good looks, desirable as they might be, are no guarantee of someone being honest, faithful, a source of strength and support, and a good provider. Instead, Chinese parents looked to the wisdom of the astrologers of old to guide them in the difficult task of seeing that their children made a good marriage.

For centuries, the ancient sages carefully studied the skies, and the movements of the sun, moon and stars, while at the same time recording what was taking place on the earth below. With the rise and fall of the celestial messengers, so they noted the triumphs and despairs of dynasties. Among their observations, they also discovered that every year has its own characteristics; and just as a vintage wine reflects the climate of the year in which it was made, so – they noticed – do the personalities of those born in that year.

This accounts for the most obvious difference between Chinese astrology and western systems. It is a special characteristic of Chinese astrology that someone's zodiac sign does not refer to the month in which that person was born, but to the year – so it is extremely difficult for a Chinese lady ever to lie about her age!

THE TWELVE ANIMALS

Each Chinese year has the name of one of twelve animals. They are the Rat, Ox, Tiger, Hare, Dragon, Snake, Horse, Sheep, Monkey, Rooster, Dog and Pig. The years run in cycles so that the same animal-year recurs every twelve years.

Because these names are translations from the Chinese, you may find variations. For example, the first sign is sometimes called the Mouse instead of the Rat; the name Buffalo or Cow is used for the second sign, instead of Ox; Rabbit for Hare; and Goat instead of Sheep. This is because the words for these alternatives are the same in Chinese. But it is wrong to call the last sign a Boar, since the Chinese word for boar is quite different from the one for Pig. And you should never, ever, call the fourth sign a Cat, as the Vietnamese do, because the Hare has a special significance for the Chinese, as you will see.

No one really knows when the animal signs were first used, nor where they came from. Two thousand years ago, they had never been heard of. Then, suddenly, round about the seventh century, the animal names cropped up in places as far apart as Turkey and Korea. Since it was at about this time that Buddhism began to spread from India, it is probable that the names were invented by Buddhist monks, who tried to make the original, complicated Chinese calendar easier to understand.

Whoever invented the names obviously hit on a good idea, because the twelve animal names suddenly became widely popular. People now had a simple, memorable system to use for counting the years, and for keeping a tally of their ages, since one's animal sign never changes.

The animal names also provided everybody with a simple guide to the basic principles of Chinese astrology. By comparing their own birth animal with that of the coming year, they would have insight into what the immediate future had in store for them. And by comparing their birth animal with that of someone else, they could identify whether they were compatible or not.

WHO ARE COMPATIBLE?

Two people can love each other, but be quite unsuitable as partners. One of the oldest legends of China tells the story of just such a young couple – a cattle herder and a weaving maid. These two were so wrapped up in each other that the weaving maid left her shuttle and loom, so there was no more cloth to sell, while the herder neglected his cattle, and they wandered off. Furious, their parents separated them and only allowed them to meet once a year. To this day, the Chinese say, the herder and the weaving maid can be seen in the night sky as two bright stars separated by the River of Heaven, known to us as the Milky Way.

The couple were certainly in love, and perhaps they even thought they were compatible; but the Chinese parents thought otherwise. Would the cattle herder have been able to support his family? Would the weaving maid have been a good mother to her children? Sometimes, alas, our hearts and our heads tell us different things.

There are, of course, different types of love. Two people may be perfect companions, and show great affection for each other; but there is no magic that binds them together inseparably. Another couple may desire each other passionately, yet be so unlike in every other respect that they seem to spend their waking hours battling furiously. Some are able to lead quite independent lives, and yet be as fond of each other as it is possible to be.

All these possibilities can be suggested by the compatibility of a couple's animal signs. The professional Chinese astrologer uses a chart of the twelve animal signs, showing the twelve signs round a clock face. Those animals which are two or four hours apart are regarded as compatible, but those which are three or six hours apart are not. A quick glance at the sample chart provided at the bottom of this page should serve to tell you whether your own birth sign and that of someone dear to you are in essence compatible.

To find your animal sign, use the General Table on page 108 if your birthday falls after February 20th. You can also use the General Table if your birthday falls before January 20th, but in this case remember to use the animal sign for the year *before* you were born. If your birthday falls between January 20th and February 20th, consult the Special Table of Animal Years on page 109 to see the date of the Chinese New Year for that year, as it is not constant.

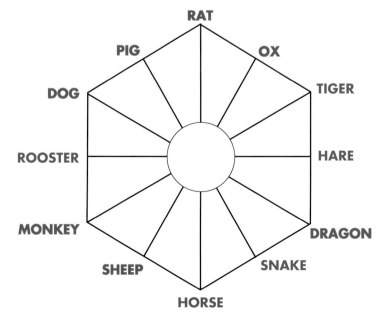

But if you and the one you have set your heart on are apparently incompatible, what can you do? Often, the presence of a third person – a child born into the marriage, perhaps – can act as the link that binds the family together. Suppose, for example, that a young couple belong to the years of the Hare and the Rooster – two animals that are diametrically opposed in the astrological chart. A child born in the years Sheep, Pig, Snake or Ox would be compatible with both its parents, and so help to stabilize the family relationship.

But whether or not partners are deemed to be compatible, the twelve animal signs can still provide a deeper insight into their relationships, and strengthen the bonds between them. A couple may have been thrown together by chance, discovering too late that there were differences in their attitudes and feelings which could not be resolved. Instead of being driven to the conclusion that they could never share their lives together, how refreshing it would be for them if they were able to identify those aspects of their individual personalities that were driving them apart! Through a deeper knowledge of each other's needs, emotions and interests, they could then learn what each expected from the other and what ought to be given in return.

Perhaps one partner is a Rat, who loves to exercise the mind and is fascinated by intricate puzzles: the other may be the convivial Horse, who longs to be outdoors. They should try to establish when they need to be together, and when they need to be apart. The Horse should realize that the Rat needs to have time to think and concentrate, while the Rat should come to appreciate the partner's dislike of being confined, understanding that search for a personal space does not mean rejection.

Or perhaps one of the couple is an exhuberant Rooster, the other a tender and affectionate Hare. It is not just a difference in ages that may create a gulf between them. Each partner typically has a

wariness, even a fear, of being misunderstood by the other. But through an understanding of their zodiacal personalities, they would learn that it is not a weakness to crave affection and reassurance, but a very basic, natural human need. Indeed, the Rooster may be only too happy to provide this, if only there were greater communication between them.

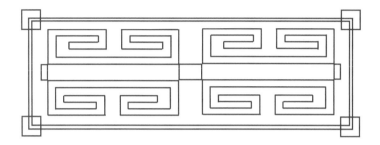

TYPES OF LOVE

Just as there are many different kinds of love which bind two people together, so there are many ways in which bonds of friendship are revealed between colleagues, companions, neighbours and family members. There are people whom we never tire of seeing, no matter how inconvenient the timing when they happen to call unexpectedly. And there are others whose constant kind attentions we must suffer uncomplainingly.

Understandably, when people speak about the compatibility between animal signs, they usually mean the relationships between two lovers; but harmony or discord may be evident in all kinds of personal relationships. Sometimes, there are strong ties of love between members of a family, and yet in spite of this there may be a complete lack of understanding on one side or the other. This has often led to serious rifts. How many tragic breakdowns have there been between one generation and the next? How many daughters have opened their hearts to their mothers, only to have their secret anxieties dismissed as insignificant? And yet in some families, mother and daughter share their most intimate confidences, acting and thinking with almost telepathic affinity.

Similarly, some sons earnestly follow in their father's footsteps – while others are only too eager to break away from the confines of the family at the first opportunity.

Character portrayals of the twelve animal signs can give parents valuable insight into their children's likely personalities. Perhaps, for example, a Monkey child has creative potential which is not recognized by the authoritarian Tiger parent. Unable to express its talents positively, the child may become resentful and frustrated. Or perhaps a Dragon parent does not realize the Dog child's characteristic need for guidance and direction, and so allows the child to become sullen and rebellious.

By comparing their own animal signs with those of their children, parents can prepare to bridge the gap between generations, gaining insight into matters that could create problems in later years. When we compare our own animal zodiac signs with those of our friends and acquaintances, we may suddenly find explanations, too, for aspects of our companions' behaviour which had formerly puzzled us.

In the past, we may have felt betrayed by someone we had once trusted as a friend; while, conversely, when we were going through a troubled period, someone we knew only casually may have proved to be a staunch ally. Although only one of the hundreds of people we meet will ever be a partner for life, the links between the signs of the Chinese animal zodiac can also reveal which of our companions are the most likely to remain within our circle of friends in years to come.

The companions of our school years will generally share our birth sign, or belong to the animal sign just before or after our own. Certainly, the most lasting bonds are those between two signs that follow each other: the Rat and Ox, Tiger and Hare, Snake and Dragon, Horse and Sheep, Monkey and Rooster, Dog and Pig.

MARRIAGE CUSTOMS

The initial step in a future marriage was always taken by the groom's parents. Whether they had in mind a particular girl or not, they would contact a marriage-broker, or go-between, who would present a token gift – usually a goose – and a red card to the parents of the prospective bride. On this card were written the man's name, and eight Chinese characters – the basic data of his horoscope. The girl's parents then had an opportunity to make a few discreet enquiries. If they thought it was worth considering the offer, they would send back a similar red card to the man's parents. Now, both sides, through the go-between, would discuss the terms of the marriage; and when this had been agreed on, there was an exchange of presents. Then the date for the marriage would be considered and, once again, the astrologer had a part to play, for the date had to be suitable astrologically to both sides.

On the auspicious day, a party from the bride-groom's family would go to the bride's house to escort her in full regalia to the groom's family home. Her wedding dress would be in the traditional red. This is considered a lucky colour; white, said to be unlucky, reminds the Chinese of funerals. The bride would now renounce her ties with her own family by paying homage to the groom's ancestors; and finally, she would signify that she was a married woman by offering ceremonial tea to all the guests. Although these ancient traditions are still carried on in many parts of China, nowadays Chinese girls often prefer to get married in white, while the formal proceedings will be recorded in a Registry Office.

Among the features of this book are the tales that introduce each of the twelve sections. These reveal a typical astrological profile of each of the twelve animal personalities, and their most compatible companions. The plots of the stories are highly relevant. The story of the Tiger, for example, is about authority; the tale of the Horse deals with the battle of the sexes; and the Pig's story is about home and family matters. Many of the tales also refer to Chinese marriage customs. The astrologer played several important roles in formalizing a marriage contract. Traditionally, he had to draw up horoscopes for the prospective couple in order to see whether they were compatible.

Chinese Love Signs may not find your perfect partner for you. But the advice this book brings can certainly help you to assess the prospects for your future happiness. Even if the right person for you happens to be the wrong person for your Chinese horoscope, you and your partner will be able to reach greater mutual understanding by learning more about each other's zodiacal personality.

If you have still not embarked on the course of true love – or are still doubtful about the best partner for you – there is still time for you to heed the advice in these twelve tales of the Chinese zodiac.

THE STORY TITLES

The titles of the twelve tales in this book are taken from traditional Chinese sayings and expressions. Brief explanations of their meanings are given below.

1. The Rat
It is hard to gather spilt water
This expression emphasizes the irreversibility of fate.

2. The Ox
True gold fears no furnace
In tough situations, virtuous qualities – here likened to true gold – should prove strong enough to survive any test, no matter how fiery, according to ancient Chinese belief.

3. The Tiger
An uninvited guest
This direct quotation from the *I Ching*, one of China's most ancient works of literature, refers to change in circumstances following the arrival of someone unexpected.

4. The Hare
Dead embers burst into flames
When the Grand Astrologer Ssu-ma Ch'ien (145-86 BC) first used this phrase in his *Historical Records*, it was with reference to the resurrection of an abandoned plan.

5. The Dragon
Retune the string, change the direction
By exploiting a particular talent, according to the sages of old, life can take a completely different turn.

6. The Snake
Too much ceremony hides deceit
The elaborate court rituals of ancient China often provided a shield for corrupt officials – hence this expression.

7. The Horse
Who's the man and who's the woman?
The Chinese sometimes use this phrase as a taunt in a situation where the stereotyped roles of the 'strong' man and 'weak' woman have become blurred.

8. The Sheep
A broken mirror is restored
This simple image – in which two halves come together again – refers to the reunification of lovers after separation.

9. The Monkey
Running water does not get stagnant
Those who are quick-thinking will constantly find themselves involved in fresh experiences, the Chinese say.

10. The Rooster
Ripples in an old well
Here, an ancient saying has been reversed in order to highlight the essence of the story. According to the T'ang dynasty poet Meng Chiao (751-814), 'There are no ripples in an old well'. As this tale clearly demonstrates, however, he was almost certainly mistaken. Passion does indeed arise in the more mature.

11. The Dog
Riding a horse to look for a horse
Sometimes, when you are searching for something – whether an object or a person – you cannot see it, even though it may be right in front of you.

12. The Pig
Building a new stove
Symbolically, this phrase refers to the starting of a new life, as occurs when a bride moves into her new home.

CHAPTER ONE

THE RAT

It is hard to gather spilt water

The broad fields glistened white in the winter sunshine. Three farm girls, securely wrapped in their padded jackets and felt boots, trudged to the farmhouse, paying no heed to the bitter cold. Squealing with delight, they picked up handfuls of the crisp, clean snow and rubbed it in each others' faces.

From the farmhouse, a reprimanding voice called out. 'What are you doing, Lei? Come here at once out of the cold! And where is the millet?'

'All finished, Mother,' Lei answered, still laughing. 'We've been trying to put colour into our complexions.'

'And what colour would that be? Blue, to judge by your faces. Come in now, girls, and sit by the kang. Get yourselves warm.'

Lei's two friends – Nali and Fo-tien – complied gladly. While it was fun in the snow, the heated, rug-covered bench where the family usually sat was certainly more welcome. Lei's mother passed her daughter a pot of hot broth.

'Give this to the girls, Lei. And when they've finished, you can ask Chia to escort them back home.'

Nali and Fo-tien immediately broke into a fit of giggling, sharing what seemed to be some private joke.

Lei's father looked up and studied them with some amusement. 'What's all that squeaking about? You sound like a lot of mice.'

'That's because we are little mice,' laughed Nali, 'all born in the year of the Rat, and all working together in the barn.'

'In that case,' said Lei's mother, guessing the reason for their merriment, 'Chia will be quite safe with you.

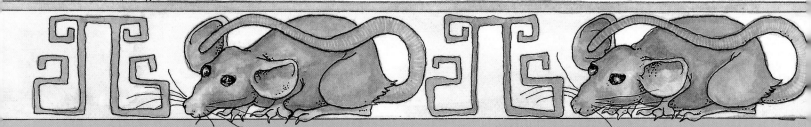

'You see, he was born in the year of the Rooster and so he is completely unsuitable for any rat or mouse that might think otherwise.'

For a moment, Nali stared at Lei's mother in astonishment. Too embarrassed to contradict her, she stifled her mirth, while her companion, Fo-tien, reddened and hid her face in her sleeve.

Lei's brother, Chia, pulled on his heavy topcoat, muttering: 'We'd better get going right away. It will soon be dark.'

Lei's mother felt a twinge of conscience. By rights, she should be accompanying the girls herself. But it would take her too long to struggle over the snow-drifts that covered the roads to their houses. Chia, on the other hand, could make his way there and back in half the time. He was sound and reliable, she tried to convince herself.

The girls had no such qualms. Before they set off, Nali pulled Lei aside and asked: 'Which of us does your brother like the best?'

Lei glanced over her shoulder as if to make sure she was not overheard. Then, to Nali's exasperation, she replied: 'He likes both of you.'

Outside, Nali gave Fo-tien a conspiratorial look. 'He likes me better,' she whispered. 'You just see.' Fo-tien smiled, but her friend's remark did not please her. Although they were the same age, Nali was much more assertive, always wanting her own way. And, it seemed, she was determined to get Chia for herself. Fo-tien felt a strange anguish that bit into her even more painfully than the sharp, cold wind.

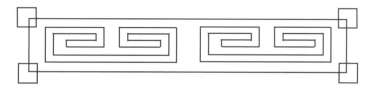

Nali had imagined that the journey home would be a leisurely stroll, with plenty of time for chatting and other pleasantries. But her hopes were dashed. Chia walked briskly through the snow, and the girls had

to force themselves to keep up with him, taking several short running steps for each of his strides. It made them breathless, and conversation was impossible. 'Not so fast, Chia,' Nali called out. 'My legs are beginning to ache. There's plenty of time before it gets dark.'

Chia stopped for a moment, and then gave Nali a penetrating look which somehow disturbed her. His voice was coaxing, yet quietly intense. 'We must hurry. We mustn't be late.' He took her hand, and Nali caught his sense of urgency. She did not reply, but responded by quickening her pace to match his. Fo-tien gritted her teeth, and stumbled on behind.

They reached Fo-tien's house first, much sooner than they were expected – to the great satisfaction of her parents. But Chia and Nali declined their invitation for hot tea, explaining that Nali wanted to get home. Fo-tien silently waved them on their way, then joined her family for the evening meal. But hungry as she had been, her appetite had now gone.

For a long time, Fo-tien sat by the window, staring across the empty fields. She should have seen Nali and Chia in the distance, making their way to Nali's house. But there was no sign of them. The fields darkened, and she fell into a fitful sleep. Suddenly, she was woken by the sound of crunching snow, as two figures slipped furtively away from the stable and scurried off into the distance.

As the truth of what had happened dawned on her, Fo-tien's agony increased. She sobbed silently into her pillow, and clenched her fists impotently, desperately afraid of waking her parents or brothers. Not that she need have fear of that – their snoring echoed through the house, proclaiming a peaceful contentment that was in glaring contrast to her own inner turmoil.

Fo-tien had lain there about an hour when, cutting through the night air, there came another sound. Fo-tien froze. It was no more than a whisper; but for

Fo-Tien, it was as deafening as a thunderclap.
'Fo-tien! It's me!'
Chia's voice filled her with both terror and ecstasy. Her heart pounded so violently, she thought that it must surely wake her father. Noiselessly, she threw her jacket round her shoulders, and went outside.

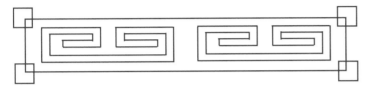

Chia's father regarded his son with bewilderment. 'You've got yourself into this mess, and now you expect me to get you out of it? Don't think I've any sympathy for you.' Chia winced as his sister put another hot, wet cloth to his face. The beating he received from one of Fo-tien's brothers had been merciless. 'You can't marry both of them,' his father said. 'But you'll have to marry one.'

His father pondered the practical aspects of the problem. 'You'd better marry Nali. Her family's got more land. In any case, to judge from the look of you, the other girl's family wouldn't want you. I expect we'll have to take care of her and her child. Woe betide us if it's another girl. Thank heavens your sister's got more sense. At least she's decided to get married before she has any children. Well, Lei, you've got yourself a nice young man, so don't keep him waiting.' Lei shyly acknowledged her father's compliment, kissed her brother lightly, and went out to the courtyard.

Jen-tang had brought her another gift – a tiny, stone snuff bottle, intricately carved with a mouse and monkey clambering over a plantain leaf. It was his own workmanship. Lei gasped in admiration.
'The mouse is meant to be you – and I am the monkey,' he explained.
'Jen-tang, this is beautiful. You are so very clever. City people would love to have things like these. Why do you waste your talents working on the farm?'

'Perhaps if you were with me to give me inspiration, we could open a shop in the city and sell my carvings.' He blushed, appalled at his presumption. 'I'd like that very much,' she replied. 'Provided that we never sell this carving.'

Events went more or less as Lei's father had foreseen. Lei's marriage to Jen-tang was happy and prosperous, and under his wife's guidance, Jen-tang became a successful artist, and his miniatures soon became highly prized collectors' items.

But the fate of Lei's brother was less than happy. He resented his marriage to Nali, and took no interest in their farm, which soon went into decline. Fo-tien's child had been a son; and despite Chia's father's offer to make amends, Fo-tien decided to stay with her own family. Although she received many offers of marriage, she refused them all.

One day, while carrying water to the house, she was startled by a familiar voice behind her.
'Fo-tien! It's me. Chia!'
She dropped the pitcher. It smashed, and the water ran into the parched ground.
'Fo-tien, I need you! Come with me. I've left Nali. I know you love me, or you'd have married by now.'

Fo-tien stared at the shattered pieces of jug, then picked them up and handed them to Chia. At first, he wondered what she was trying to do. Then he realized the significance of the broken pitcher and the spilt water. With a cry of despair, he threw the pieces to the ground and walked away.

Once he had gone, Fo-tien turned and walked back to the house.
'We need a new water-pitcher, father.'
The old man grunted an acknowledgement.
'I've been thinking, father. The marriage-broker you mentioned...'
Her father looked up expectantly.
'The next time he calls,' Fo-tien said, 'tell him...tell him...nothing.'

The Rat personality

The Rat, or the even humbler mouse – the Chinese word is the same for both – may seem a strange leader for the twelve animals of the Chinese zodiac; yet the choice is very apt, for the Rat personality is both complex and sensitive. Ambitious, yet afraid of being thought overbearing, the Rat's unique talents may lie undiscovered until it is almost too late. If Rat-types are lucky enough to move in the right circles early in life, however, they can soon collect a coterie of admirers to boost their self-confidence. But without the devoted help of able partners at their side, to give guidance and encouragement when it is most needed, they may end up isolated and despondent.

Rat personalities have good, creative minds, and are excellent at getting things started. But they are hopeless finishers, and many of their best ideas come to nothing for want of determination to finalize their schemes. They no sooner get a project started than they tend to want to begin on something else.

People may often form immediate judgements of the Rat – some find the Rat's manner charming and agreeable, while others may take an instant dislike to someone who appears so insincere.

Both these opinions have some foundation, but neither is entirely right. It is the Rat's need to push forward, to direct others towards a specific goal – whether they want this or not – which makes both friends and enemies.

Rat personalities are often of a philosophical turn of mind, interested in obscure subjects, and are mines of useless information, with a fondness for crosswords and mathematical puzzles. Strangely, however, this ability to juggle words and figures does not extend to practical, everyday life. Financially, they ought to be very adept at handling their budgets – yet, while they have no difficulty in managing other people's finances for them, they treat their own accounts with disdain. They tend to save for months on end, and then go on wild spending sprees without any thought for the consequences.

Ancient Chinese astrologers also chose the nocturnal Rat to represent the midnight hour; and indeed, many Rat personalities do seem suddenly to come alive late at night. This can mean an exciting love-life for those who become the partners of Rat personalities, particularly if their passions are also likely to come to the fore after midnight has struck.

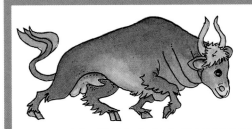
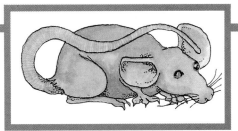

WHO IS THE PERFECT PARTNER FOR THE RAT?

The Rat makes friends easily; and the more ardent Rat has no difficulty in finding lovers for casual relationships. But a deeper relationship – for support, understanding and mutual trust – is a different matter. Few people really get to the heart of the Rat's true personality; and even when in an apparently stable, loving relationship, there may be part of the Rat's life that remains isolated and insecure.

Perhaps no one would be a more suitable life companion than the dependable Ox. Ever-patient, and ready to help when most needed, the Ox can in turn benefit from the Rat's stimulating presence and enthusiasm, which adds a richness to the Ox partner's life.

But if the Rat has no inclination to settle down, preferring a life of adventure and excitement, then either the exotic Dragon or the daring Monkey would be ideal. Together, their lives would be that much more full.

At the other extreme, a Rat is not likely to gain much from a relationship with a Horse personality. Though the Horse might seem to be able to offer the Rat a steadying influence, as well as an adventurous spirit, there is something in this relationship that does not quite strike true. It is often some time before the problem is revealed – and by then, both partners may have learned to cope with it.

More suitable life companions for the Rat would be the Tiger or Dog personalities. The Tiger is likely to offer financial security; the Dog, practical help. Though they may have sharply opposing opinions on certain topics, such partners have enough in common to forge a warm and loving relationship.

How each of the twelve personality types
relates to the Rat

With ANOTHER RAT

Most couples who are born under the same sign are compatible, but there is often friction when two Rat personalities are together. Both are very determined characters, and each prefers to take the lead. Indeed, if they share the same household, there is often a conflict of interests as neither partner will be content to take a secondary role in the relationship. But this desire always to take the initiative can make for a very exciting love-life. When matters are going well, theirs is certainly a stimulating relationship. But, sadly, the partnership is frequently a brittle one.

With THE OX

The Rat's positive characteristics are leadership, creativity and eagerness; but there is a tendency for enthusiasm to wither unless the rewards are within close reach. This is why the support of the Ox is so valuable, providing encouragement and practical help. In everyday life, the Rat is likely to be the inspiration and enthusiasm behind any decisions, although the Ox is more likely to be the one left to attend to all the practical details. Where romance is concerned, the Rat is the spark which the Ox fans into a fire. Even when it might seem that the embers are dying, the Ox can coax fresh life into the relationship.

With THE TIGER

A relationship between the energetic Rat and the glamour-loving Tiger is often a tempestuous one. Yet they both understand each other's needs, and have no illusions regarding their position in the relationship. The Rat is held fast by the Tiger's magnetic charisma; and the Tiger needs the Rat's strong support and encouragement. To outsiders, they may appear self-sufficient, leading separate, fulfilling lives, but they are well aware of their own limitations and their dependence on each other. This relationship strengthens as the couple learn more about each other.

With THE HARE

The Rat's charm seems to be at its least apparent when the partner is a Hare. Taking the Hare's trusting affection too much for granted, the Rat may treat the Hare cavalierly – an attitude that cannot last forever. The Hare should not be intimidated, however; nor should he or she be afraid to leave the Rat if the situation becomes unmanageable. The Rat will soon realize how valuable the relationship has been, and separation will not be for long. However, if the Rat can learn to treat the Hare with consideration, and the Hare can accept the Rat's casual manner with patience, this partnership has a good chance of survival.

With THE DRAGON

For complete fulfilment, the Rat is unlikely to find a better choice of partner than the Dragon. Unfortunately, however, there is often a lack of practicality in this relationship, which combines intelligence with talent, but is short on realism and common sense. Nevertheless, if there is a target which they can both aim for, they will make a formidable team. Whatever their objective – career advancement, material comforts, or fame – together, they will achieve it. Their physical love is passionate and fulfilling, often with extravagant displays of affection.

With THE SNAKE

The Snake is not an easy partner for the Rat. Learned astrologers might pore over their charts and merely declare that the two are neither compatible nor hostile; but ordinary folk might not be so optimistic, pointing out that snakes eat rats! However, despite everyone's warnings, the Rat is likely to fall for the Snake's alluring charms in a big way. So it is up to the Rat to keep a cool head and stand firm – for it is not just finances which could be in danger. The Rat's special individuality, too, may only too easily be swallowed up by the Snake's powerfully energetic personality.

18

With THE HORSE

These two contrasting partners are often thrown together by force of circumstances. If the Rat is the older partner, it is often the case that the relationship began at a time when the Horse was in a very vulnerable position, and the Rat felt close sympathy which developed into a kind of love. But as time passes, the Horse character often strengthens, eventually dominating the Rat. When the Horse is the older partner, more often than not the dominant role played by the Horse is evident right from the start. But as neither partner likes to take a subservient role, this is why problems could sometimes begin. Very clearly defined rules are necessary for this partnership, if it is to succeed and prove long-lasting.

With THE SHEEP

This is one of the more uncommon relationships for the Rat; and a shared interest in some activity, hobby or occupation is more likely to have brought these two together rather than mere sexual attraction. Indeed, it was probably a while before the two acknowledged their fondness for each other, and mutual passion may have come as a surprise to both of them. Once they step outside overtly shared interests, however, they may eventually find it difficult to communicate. And although passion may drift away, the mutual need for companionship will always remain and help to keep them together, even if they occasionally seem to have a roving eye.

With THE MONKEY

If the Rat partner is female, this could be the ideal relationship; but even for Mr Rat, the Monkey makes one of the best choices of partner he could possibly make. The two succeed because they can both bring special gifts to the partnership. With the Rat's creative flair and the Monkey's more practical attitude to everyday matters, they make an excellent team. Together, their remarkable talents might even take them to the top. Their shared sense of adventure and fun will also add spice and delight to the physical side of their love; and they should have a long, busy, and happy life ahead of them.

With THE ROOSTER

The words 'peaceful coexistence' do not come readily to mind when the Rat and Rooster join forces. Both these zodiacal animals are extremely active personalities, demanding excitement and change. Theirs is, therefore, a relationship that works best when both partners are allowed to have time and space of their own. They must be allowed to develop their own potential. If they feel too strongly bound to each other through a misplaced sense of loyalty or other obligations, they may easily come to resent the resulting loss of individuality. The romantic relationship between these two is frequently very much an on-and-off affair. Strangely, though, the more often they break up, the longer, it seems, they are likely to stay together in the end.

With THE DOG

The Rat may feel uncomfortable and intimidated by a Dog partner; but once the initial distrust has gone, these two can become extremely close. Unfortunately, the negative side of one partner is often accentuated by the other, though each soon becomes familiar with the partner's changing moods, and – in time – learns how to cope. The Rat may not like the Dog's open frankness, and the Dog may resent the Rat's preference for privacy. To find a solution, compromise is obviously the keyword here.

With THE PIG

This contented couple would be very surprised if you told them that they were not ideal for one another. Against all odds, they frequently settle down and have a happy home together, ignoring all the advice of parents, friends, and perhaps even counsellors. Often in this relationship, the Rat is the younger, male partner, happy to allow himself to be fussed over, and to be put in his place, by a dominant, but not domineering, Pig. Surprisingly, there is likely to be more romance in this relationship than is apparent to the outside observer. As for the physical side of their love, to judge from the evidence – frequently, a large and close family – this would appear to be perfectly satisfactory for both.

CHAPTER TWO

THE OX

True gold fears no furnace

The marshal in charge of the royal escort looked at the darkening skies with dismay. 'We can't go on, Mr Kiu,' he announced grimly to the Master of the Household. 'Will you let His Highness know the news?'

'And collect our death warrants at the same time?' Mr Kiu replied. There was no humour in his voice.

In the first of the carriages, the Lady Ming-loi shifted her position wearily. A charcoal burner ensured that the carriage was kept warm, but it made the air stuffy and uncomfortable. Lady Ming-loi's companion, the Lady Ta-ti, lifted the leather curtain slightly to let in some fresh air, but the draught was bitingly cold, and she soon fastened it tightly once again.

The weather was not their only trial. Although both ladies wore travelling clothes, these were elegant, rather than practical. The Lady Ming-loi, for example, found that the gold-and-jade trimmings of her dress bit painfully into her skin, adding to the catalogue of troubles that marked this ill-fated journey. Inwardly, she cursed herself for not having had the courage to stand up to her father and his counsellors. But despite her royal blood, she was still no more than a cog in the machinery of state.

It suited the Imperial Will that she marry the Prince Jang-tan to strengthen links with a distant province. That, apparently, was her destiny. It did not matter that she might never see her family again, nor that the people she would govern did not speak her language.

The intended marriage between the Lady Ming-loi and Prince Jang-tan was not a match favoured by the Grand Astrologer. Prince Jang-tan was born in the year of the Snake. It was therefore considered disastrous for him to marry someone, such as the Lady Ming-loi, born in the year of the Pig. But Grand Astrologers do not attain their exalted positions by contradicting the decrees of their superiors.

Instead, he announced that a third party – whose horoscope harmonized with those of the Prince and the Lady Ming-loi – would ensure the stability of the union. This third party, he advised, would be their future child. But until then, the Prince and his bride would need to rely on the services of a mutual confidante of suitable rank and breeding, to act as a mediator should discord arise.

A suitable confidante would be born in the year of the Rooster, the astrologer advised. Unfortunately, this left him with the painful task of explaining to the Master of the Household that, although he was born in the auspicious year of the Rooster, his rank, exalted though it was, did not equate with royal kinship. So, instead, a courtier, the Lady Ta-ti, was chosen. She was born in a Rooster year which fell some twelve years later than the rubicund Mr Kiu's. The Lady Ming-loi took to the Lady Ta-ti because she had an artistic flair, knew all the card games, and was in touch with the world outside the court.

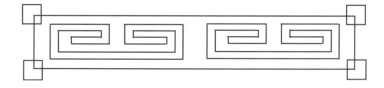

Mr Kiu looked out through a slit in the blinds. More snow, and it was getting dark. He called to an outrider.
'Tell His Highness that we are obliged to make camp here.'
When the old farmer saw the troops of soldiers and servants approach the house, his first instinct was to hide anything of value in the cellar, though a couple of kitchen utensils and a few jars of pickles could hardly be regarded as treasure. Children watched open-mouthed as horses, banners, soldiers, and – most wonderful of all – carriages approached.

There was a heavy banging at the door. Fearfully, the farmer nodded to his eldest daughter, Ni-erh, a woman of some forty years. She had an abundance of the qualities that typify those born in the year of the Ox – a powerful physique and commanding personality. These, sad to say, were heavily disguised blessings, for long ago she had frightened off many a would-be suitor, and was now resigned to remaining unmarried.

Ni-erh lifted the heavy bolt. The door was immediately flung open by a man of generous proportions, dressed in the finest clothes she had ever seen. But her awe was shattered as soon as he spoke.
'I have to tell you that we are commandeering your house for the night.'
His trilling voice was so unexpected that Ni-erh burst out laughing. With a disdainful sniff, he brushed past her, and addressed her father.

'We have our own provisions. This will more than compensate you for your trouble.'

He tipped a couple of gold pieces on to the table. The farmer stared at them in disbelief. Then, misinterpreting the farmer's silence, the Master of the Household threw down a few more pieces, adding: 'That's all you're getting.'

Ni-erh, realizing that her parents were too shocked to be of any practical help, swept up the gold pieces and put them into her father's pocket. A porter had brought some fur rugs from the carriages. Without ceremony, she snatched one, and ushered her family into the storeroom.

Within a short while, a handful of people from the royal escort stood in the tiny farmhouse, looking about them, perplexed. As they seemed to be at a loss, Ni-erh took over. She stoked up the fire, placed an iron cauldron on top, and tipped water into it. She then gave directions to a manservant.

'Go outside and get more wood for the fire. Do you have food? Then bring it. Put your men in the cow-shed. These women can stay here.'

Mr Kiu waved his arms impotently. All the servants caught on quickly, saying: 'Yes, Sir. Right away, Sir,' in response to Kiu's directions, but following Ni-erh's orders instead. She dismissed the porter who had brought the rugs, then handed them to two women who appeared to be in charge.

'Make your beds up over there,' she ordered, 'and then give me a hand chopping these turnips.'

The women's mouths dropped open, and they appealed to someone who had just come in. Ni-erh turned and saw a pale young man standing in the doorway.

'And you – if you want to make yourself useful, get over to the cow-shed and start putting down straw.'

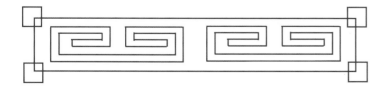

It was another two days before the Prince and the two ladies, all now sharing a carriage, were able set off on their journey again. During their time at the farmhouse, they had not been idle. Ni-erh had seen to that.

'It was when she commanded me to go to the cow-shed!' said the Lady Ming-loi. 'If I live my life a thousand times, nothing will ever match that! What an absolute gem she was. You know, when I get to Shansi, I'm going to make it a rule that all court ladies do their own washing.'

The Prince grinned with happiness, and kissed both ladies lightly in turn. The Lady Ming-loi smiled. 'I'll be a good wife to you,' she said to the Prince. 'Just wait and see. And will you let Ta-ti stay after our child is born?'

'I think Ta-ti may want to make arrangements of her own, or was that court business I saw her discussing with that handsome officer? Don't worry, I'm sure we can find a suitable position for him at court, too,' he reassured her.

'Talking of positions at court,' queried the Lady Ming-loi, 'What is going to happen to that extraordinary woman? We really owe our lives, and also our happiness, to her.'

'I asked her what she wanted,' the Prince answered the future First Lady, 'and her request was simple – so I granted it.'

Further behind in the procession, Ni-erh sat proudly in her grand carriage, the leather curtains drawn back. Fortune, she thought, was a strange thing. A week ago, she had been approaching middle age, and never a hope of marrying. All the fine clothes in the world would not make her young again, but at least she now had a husband.

The man shivering opposite her sneezed.

'Oh, you poor soul,' she said tenderly. 'You're cold.' She patted his shoulder gently and closed the blinds.

'Thank you, my dear,' said the Master of the Household, weakly, 'You're so considerate.'

The Ox personality

The Ox is remarkable for strength, both physical and of purpose. Whether male or female, Ox personalities are also generally much better finishers than innovators. They therefore tend to be the builders and developers of the world, able to follow plans through to their conclusion. They are unlikely to be influenced by criticism, though may proceed with caution at first. Once they are sure that they have hit on the right course, however, it will take a lot to persuade them otherwise.

Ox personalities are naturally sociable, but prefer to stay within an established circle. They may not make new friends easily, but it will not be for want of trying. Often lacking experience in dealing with people from other cultures or walks of life, they may find communication awkward. But they tend to compensate for this failing by appearing self-assured and over-confident – sometimes, even uncaring and aggressive. However, the Ox's inner nature is usually much more compassionate than is apparent.

In general, Ox personalities have little difficulty in reaching the highest positions in their careers – characteristically through determination and sheer force of personality.

The Ox leads, not so much by example, but by pushing others into place. They can also be hard-headed business people; but, true to character, usually prefer to stick to tried and trusted methods, and are suspicious of new technology.

Perhaps one of the Ox personality's most endearing characteristics is a love of fun. However, while those who enjoy hearty, boisterous company will be happy to have the Ox for a partner, more sensitive types may find the Ox's fondness for practical jokes irritating at times. The typical Ox-type also likes to be active and outdoors – the open air and physical well-being are crucial to the health-conscious Ox. This physicality, however, does not always extend to competitive sports.

Despite an earthy sense of humour, the Ox's approach to love, romance and the sexual side of a relationship is, on the whole, surprisingly conventional. Indeed, the Ox may already have several deep-seated prejudices about personal relationships, loyalty and the role that each partner plays. Unfortunately, any attempts to persuade the Ox that these opinions might be ill-founded – and even perhaps out-dated – often lead to suspicion and resentment.

WHO IS THE PERFECT PARTNER FOR THE OX?

Whoever decides to take on the Ox personality as a partner must be ready for a lifetime commitment. For though the Ox may be slow to enter into a serious relationship, there is no turning back once this has been decided on. However, there may be several casual liaisons before any binding vows are made; and until then, Ox-types are unlikely to consider themselves under any obligation of fidelity.

Those who claim to prefer open relationships should therefore avoid getting tied to people born in the year of the Ox. Not only will their Ox partners be heavily possessive, but they can also make fearsome enemies. Though the patience of the Ox is proverbial, it would be foolhardy to put it to the test. Indeed, the Ox is said to be the only zodiac sign that is able to overcome the Tiger – usually the most formidable of opponents.

Some partners may find that, in romance, the Ox's attitude is very basic – earthy, even; and this may be a characteristic that does not suit those who prefer a more refined approach or who wish to be a little more experimental in lovemaking. But on the credit side, the Ox will never be ashamed to reveal any inner feelings. Should the Ox ever doubt the partner's fidelity, the partner will be the first to know about it. And if there are doubts about the physical side of the relationship, the Ox will be frank and forthright.

The most suitable partner for the Ox is undoubtedly another Ox, since they are likely to find communication easy. But for someone to bring variety and spice into the Ox's life, the ideal partner would be either the studious and graceful Snake or the exuberant Rooster. The Pig, meanwhile, will be affectionate and supportive.

How each of the twelve personality types relates to the Ox

With THE RAT

If the Ox – who is usually the dominant figure in any relationship – does not mind taking a secondary role, then this match between Ox and Rat could be ideal. Some might think the Rat stands to benefit most, leaning too heavily on the supportive Ox, but in fact the Ox gains considerably from the Rat's special gifts and capabilities: the Rat gives some edge to a life that might otherwise be rather routine. The partnership is likely to be rich and fulfilling, with a strong physical element adding to their compatibility.

With ANOTHER OX

Two Ox-types will be perfectly happy together. Each will feel confident and assured in the other's presence, and will have an instinctive feel for the other's needs. The only drawback to this strong relationship is that it may make them exclusive: the difficulty that the Ox sometimes has in communicating with outsiders is intensified by sharing a life with someone who has equally restricted interests. Physically, as well as emotionally, compatible, the two Ox-types are very responsive to each other, and show little reluctance in speaking frankly about any worries or problems that arise concerning their most intimate moments.

With THE TIGER

'One Ox can conquer two Tigers', runs an old Chinese proverb, meaning that even the charismatic Tiger is obliged to take second place to the forceful Ox. Initial attraction between Ox and Tiger may well be purely physical. Indeed, their personalities are so different that – in any long-term relationship – they may possibly end up leading separate lives. As this is not a situation that the Ox personality cares for, it can lead to jealousy and friction. Despite the Ox being a *yin* (feminine) sign, and the Tiger a *yang* (masculine) one, this is a relationship that works best when the Ox is allowed to be the dominant partner.

With THE HARE

Whether male or female, the Hare brings a touch of tenderness and romance into the Ox's life. Such a couple will be devoted to each other. The Ox is protective and supportive, providing physical and material help; and the Hare gives psychological reassurance when times are hard. There is a strong bond of understanding between them, even though their interests may actually be quite different. For once, the Ox may be prepared to listen to someone else's views. Family life will be stable and contented, providing an environment that is full of affection for any children.

With THE DRAGON

On the face of it, these are two determined types who know what they want, and have carefully assessed the consequences of getting involved. But what seems ideal on the surface may not work in practice. No one can explain, for instance, why, in this relationship, a partner's presence is welcome one moment, and resented the next. There may also be a lack of direction, especially where financial matters are concerned, since both partners may have different priorities. Their love-life could be marked by moments of bliss, but also by long stretches of inactivity.

With THE SNAKE

The Snake personality makes an ideal partner for the Ox. Here are two people who are willing to make a commitment to each other, even if this means some personal sacrifice – such as leaving a home town or country, or giving up a career. But the gains are likely to provide more than adequate recompense. Although few couples are so different in character, they have a mysterious rapport, binding them together. Indeed, they may have entirely different interests, but each finds that the other is able to supply something that has been missing in the other's life.

With THE HORSE

The Ox and Horse seem destined to hit it off from the start, but frequently find that they lose interest in one another. The danger, at the beginning, is in expecting too much of the partner, with the Ox trying to mould the Horse according to particular ideals which the Horse is neither willing, nor able, to support. The biggest problem in this relationship is boredom; but if the partnership can last long enough for children to be born, it has a greater chance of survival. Their love-life has an earthy passion, but it lacks the essential ingredients of romance and surprise. In time, the physical side of the relationship may grow less attractive or important, so there needs to be another aspect to their companionship which can yoke these two together.

With THE SHEEP

In choosing a Sheep, a difficult time could lie ahead for the unsuspecting Ox. Indeed, it is a grave mistake for the Ox to take the Sheep for granted; for, although, at first, the Sheep may seem to be a loyal and supportive partner, there may be an undercurrent of resentment seething beneath that calm exterior. When decisions have to be made about the home, work, or leisure, the Ox must be careful to discuss everything with the Sheep partner – and even then, the Ox should consider whether the Sheep responded willingly or under pressure. When it comes to the physical side of love, it is very important for the Ox to show every possible consideration for the Sheep's sensitivity.

With THE MONKEY

Although not ideal, a partnership between an Ox and Monkey has a lot in its favour. The Monkey can bring a little colour into the Ox personality's life, while the Ox is able to give the Monkey valuable practical support, as well as sensible advice when it is most needed. It is unusual for this couple to have fallen in love at first sight – mutual affection generally grows over a period of time. Although their interests are quite different, the Ox and Monkey are likely to be drawn together by circumstances that could only be resolved through their mutual co-operation.

With THE ROOSTER

This is a fulfilling relationship for both the Ox and the Rooster. They are each able to provide something to enhance the other's quality of life: the Rooster brings excitement and flair; the Ox, steadfastness. And because the Rooster has an adventurous nature, and the Ox a more conservative one, family life is likely to be stable, but never dull. The couple's love-life is likely to be both passionate and romantic, and one which many others may well envy.

With THE DOG

The old expression 'a dog in a manger' has its counterpart in Chinese, but the symbolism is rather different. Indeed, in this relationship, it is the Ox – not the Dog – who is obstructive, preventing Dog personalities from getting what they want. As the sages of ancient times found, people born in the years of the Dog and the Ox have similar problems. What is more, the Dog personality may want to strike up a friendship with the Ox, but the Ox will find it extremely hard to respond positively. If this relationship fails, it is usually because the Ox is mistrustful and suspicious of the Dog, rather than the reverse. If the partnership is to last for any length of time, the Ox has to be much more demonstrative and caring, as well as less suspicious of the Dog's motives.

With THE PIG

There are very positive aspects to this relationship. Family life is important to both the Pig and the Ox, as are qualities such as stability and loyalty. Both personality types are aware of the need to be supportive in facing the outside world, and realize that two people joining forces can make greater progress than an individual alone. Excitement and novelty may not be as important to this couple as a secure future; and, although their ambitions may be relatively modest, they will be as successful in their careers as they will be in their family life. Romance may not be much in evidence in this relationship, but there will, nevertheless, be a strong attachment between the Ox and the Pig, due to mutual and sincere affection. Their love is reflected in a close family life.

CHAPTER THREE
THE TIGER

An uninvited guest

'Bean curd?' queried the Widow Yuan, closely examining the figures before her.

'Fifteen cart loads,' replied Sheng, her steward, checking off his list.

'Ox hides?'

'Only one cart-load, following your instructions.'

'With the twenty baskets of dried fish, that should clear the New Year debts. See that the carts are sent to the Governor's trading-house immediately. Anything else, Sheng?'

'That's all today's commercial business. But Mr San-tzu, the merchant from Tang-chiang, is here again.' The steward paused before adding quietly: 'It may be a personal matter.'

The Widow Yuan frowned, rose from her desk and peered through the lattice into the adjoining room.

'Another suitor? For me or my daughter?'

The steward shook his head, as if to say he did not know. The Widow Yuan ordered the visitor to be shown in. He was well dressed, and – she surmised – probably about her own age. He seemed a person of some importance.

'San-tzu Fen, Madame!' Sheng announced.

The Widow Yuan knew neither the name nor the face, but something about the man struck her as vaguely familiar. However, guided by intuition and ruled by etiquette, she left her curiosity to be satisfied at a time that would be more appropriate. For the moment, she confined herself to a few formal courtesies, first acknowledging the visitor's New Year greetings.

'My steward has given me your name, and tells me you are from Tang-chiang. The gardens there must be extremely beautiful now that the first flowers are beginning to show.'

The visitor bowed in acknowledgement.

'Everywhere is beautiful in Spring,' he said. 'The air is fresh, the river sparkles, and our thoughts turn to the happy days of our youth.'

The Widow sighed inwardly. This was not, she mused, the usual preamble of someone wishing to trade dried fish for timber. She ordered tea, and the conversation wafted gently along its course.

Marriage was touched upon so frequently, and yet so inconclusively, that the Widow soon began to lose patience.

'And how many wives did you say you have had?' she queried absently, at one point.

'Just the two,' replied the merchant, unaware that there might have been a touch of sarcasm in her tone. 'Unfortunately, both ladies passed away, for different reasons, quite soon after we had been married.'

'Two wives is more than most men manage in a lifetime,' replied the Widow, tartly. 'And yet you incline to a third?'

The merchant looked startled.

'Indeed no, you misunderstand. When I spoke of marriage, I was referring to my son,' he explained hastily. For a moment, he seemed to be at a loss for words, but then continued: 'Although, of course, I am sure that I have many more years left to my life, and it would be pleasant to share these with a congenial companion.'

'I have only had the privilege of one husband,' said the Widow. 'Being a Tiger myself, you can imagine that finding even one was a difficult enough task. But I was eventually fortunate enough to be married to a man who was an ideal example of those born in the year of the Horse – honest, hard-working, and a truly loving husband. I hope my daughter is equally successful. But as she too is a Tiger, so my problems begin again. You know the saying: Never bring a Tiger into the house.'

While she was talking, her visitor played with his fingers in a way that the Widow Yuan found extremely irritating. He gave an oily smile. 'There is another saying,' he ventured: 'One Ox can conquer two Tigers. Now, someone, such as myself, who has an Ox for a son, might look on such a match with great favour – the more so if the two families were operating business concerns which could be of mutual benefit'.

The Widow Yuan pushed her cup aside and studied her visitor with greater interest. It seemed the afternoon was not going to be wasted after all.

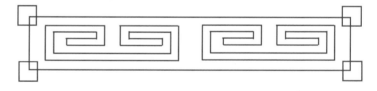

As it was the New Year, it was convenient for the Widow Yuan to invite Mr San-tzu and his son for the celebrations. Her daughter, Lan-lan, and her cousins had been hanging up spring lanterns, and it seemed an opportune moment to suggest that Lan-lan and Yun, Mr San-tzu's son, take a walk round the garden on their own. The two parents kept a discreet eye on them from their vantage point in a garden pavilion, while enjoying a dish of green crabs in ginger sauce.

Yun strode ahead with a wide grin across his face. He certainly could not fault his father's choice.

'So that's it, then,' he announced, very pleased with himself. 'I'll tell my father that I'll marry you.'

'And suppose I want to marry someone else?'

'It's not up to you. My father's loaded. Your mother wants the timber business. Anyway, you couldn't marry anyone else, even if you wanted to. Your mother would see to that.'

Lan-lan did her best not to cry. She stooped to pick up some of the broken flower heads, and carefully hid them among the foliage. As they neared the pavilion where their parents were waiting, Yun crossed the garden with the sun behind him. For a brief moment, the Widow Yuan saw him in silhouette, and for a moment found herself thirty years back in time.

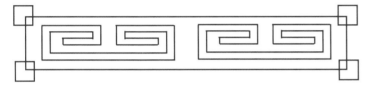

The older cousin crept over to Lan-lan's bed, and shook her gently. 'Wake up, Lan-lan. Sheng's outside.' Lan-lan turned, and rubbed her eyes. They were red from crying. 'You can talk to him through the fence,' her cousin whispered.

A voice called softly.

Lan-lan clung to the fence, unable to speak, so great was her joy and her grief.

'Lan-lan, I'll always love you, whatever happens.' Finger-tips pushed through a crack in the fence. Lan-lan grasped them and kissed them passionately. 'I can't marry him!' she cried. 'I want to be with you. If I can't, I'd rather die.'

'No Lan-lan. Please don't say that. If you died, I'd have nothing to live for.'

Suddenly, Lan-lan's cousin shouted out in alarm. There were other voices, and the sound of running footsteps. At the other side of the fence, there was a scuffle, a cry of pain, and Yun's voice calling, 'I've got him, father.'

Since the whole household was now awake, Mrs Yuan thought that the matter might as well be dealt with speedily. She summoned everyone to her counting-house.

Lan-lan sat expressionless. Mr San-tzu tried to maintain an air of dignified grievance, while his son gloated triumphantly. At the centre of the group stood the steward, Sheng, his face bloody and swollen from the beating he had received.

'May I say, Widow Yuan, that in spite of what has happened tonight, we are still prepared to stand by our proposal of marriage. Of course, there are certain conditions which will now have to be met. But I think you will find that my conditions are not only fair, but very attractive.'

'And what would these conditions be?' asked Mrs Yuan, coldly.

'Well, to begin with, I would expect your steward to be brought before the magistrate, dismissed, and replaced by someone whom I find more reliable.'

'I see. And regarding the business contract?'

'You will forgive my being presumptious, but I think it would be in the best interests of both of us if we were to seal the business contract with a more personal bond – one of marriage.'

The widow smiled. 'You are very generous, Mr San-Tzu. I should like to repay your kind proposal by giving you my answer – the opposite of the one which I gave you thirty years ago. Then, after I said "Yes" and you had your pleasure of me, you deserted both me and your family.

'As for my trusted steward Sheng, I will indeed take him to the magistrate, but only to show him the injuries received in that unprovoked attack. Unless, of course, you are prepared to offer him some recompense.'

'And as for you, young lady, I always thought that Sheng was a bit old for you, but if he's a Dragon, you'd better take the offer while it's there. The details can wait till tomorrow. Get away with you, child. No more kisses. No more kisses, I said.'

The Tiger personality

The Tiger was chosen by the Chinese astrologers of old to represent a personality that was ambitious, fearless and competitive. But being born in the year of the Tiger can be a benefit or a burden, depending on your situation in life. If you have been born into a wealthy family, or privileged place in society, having Tiger qualities will almost certainly help you to maintain your position, and to use authority effectively. But for those whose background is more humble, or disadvantaged, Tiger qualities sometimes can lead to resentment and rebelliousness. If this dissatisfaction with life's circumstances is channelled positively, however, the Tiger can be a militant champion of people's rights. But, unfortunately, such crusading zeal is not always coupled with the practical means, or the experience, to carry out a task of this kind.

Social standing is vitally important to Tiger personalities – they love to be seen with all the trappings of the good life. A failing may therefore be an inclination to give priority to what most people might regard as luxuries rather than necessities: Tigers are frequently prepared to make sacrifices at home in order to enjoy the prestige of a fast car, designer clothes, and holidays in fashionable resorts.

Tigers expect to be at the forefront of society, and if they are not born into the front rank, they will claw their way up through sheer force of personality. They also instinctively know their own weaknesses, and will compensate for them by developing some other aspect of their character, be it conversation, looks or style.

Tigers are highly capable, too, with very strong organizational skills that allow them easily to take the helm. Able to work under pressure, they make excellent managers. They are often charismatic figures, with a gift for drawing together many separate, and perhaps opposing, factions, thereby creating order where once chaos reigned.

Because the Tiger's personality displays traditional masculine values, the Chinese have always looked with disfavour on prospective wives born in a Tiger year, fearing that they will bring discord into a home. But the Tigress need have no such fear, for her personality is just as magnetic as that of any male born in the same year. And with the right partner, she can be transformed into an elegant and supportive companion, whose naturally ambitious nature can be a valuable asset to the relationship.

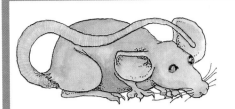

WHO IS THE PERFECT PARTNER FOR THE TIGER?

The Tiger is magnetic and vital, but it is important to remember that its dominating personality can be trying at times. Whoever takes on a Tiger as a partner must, therefore, be prepared for someone who demands constant support. This is not a task that suits everybody. The Monkey personality, for example, is too independent by nature to be a lackey. The Snake may try to please, but there is something about the Snake that arouses suspicion, and the Tiger is always likely to mistrust its ingratiating manner. The Pig personality, meanwhile, finds it difficult to share the Tiger's enthusiasm, believing that the realities of the moment are more important than the visions of tomorrow. But, if there is one partner for the Tiger to avoid above all, it must be the Ox – for it is said to be the only animal that can subdue the Tiger. Some prospective partners may also be deterred by the Tiger's love of the good life; for what the Tiger may consider an occasional luxury may be construed as extravagance.

For some people, however, the Tiger's vibrant personality is a constant source of stimulus and inspiration. Horse personalities recognize the Tiger's finer qualities, and often become loyal companions, offering practical help when they can. In love, the Tiger's dynamism is translated into ardent desire. In love, the Tiger also shows honesty and sincerity. These characteristics are most appreciated by the Dog, for whom trust and faithfulness are paramount.

With the Horse or the Dog for a partner, therefore, as well as the Rat, even female Tiger personalities – who, in China, traditionally have a hard time finding husbands – can look forward to a satisfying relationship filled with romance and passion.

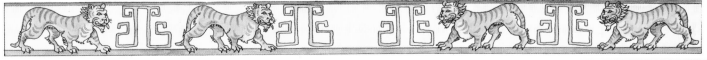

How each of the twelve personality types relates to the Tiger

With THE RAT

The Tiger will find the Rat personality is a dependable partner, whether in a business relationship or as a life companion. The Rat is supportive at home, and a valuable ally in matters of career. Both Rat and Tiger are leaders in their own ways, and recognize each other's talents without feeling competitive. This produces a strong bond of respect between them, not weakened by the independent lives they sometimes appear to lead. Their love-life may not display constant romance and passion, but both are happily fulfilled.

With THE OX

Perhaps not the best companion for the Tiger, the Ox is nevertheless one of the few personalities who can keep the Tiger under control. In the event of disagreements, the Ox will not be intimidated by the Tiger, even when power is at stake. Instead, the Ox will keep to its principles, refusing to give an inch until the Tiger submits. Their personalities are so different that the Tiger would prefer their lives to be divided into distinct areas, a situation which the Ox is bound to reject. Whether the Tiger is the male or female partner, this relationship works best when the Tiger is willing to let the Ox take the lead, or avoids placing the Ox under any kind of obligation.

With ANOTHER TIGER

This relationship can work very well, and is one that suits the Tiger personality better than any other. Both partners are strong and independent, and each recognizes the other's needs for individuality. There is companionship, but the depth of feeling between them is often left unspoken, which can be disappointing. They should realize, however, that, although they are individuals, a truly harmonious partnership only comes about when they have learnt that sharing means accepting, as well as giving. This is something that the proud and generous Tiger may be reluctant to face.

With THE HARE

Perhaps unexpectedly, this is one of the Tiger's most successful relationships. Although, logically, it would seem to be the better arrangement when the Tiger is the male partner, in fact it makes no difference to the relationship: the tendency, however, is for the Tiger to lead and the Hare to follow. Outwardly, no couple could be more unevenly matched, but each personality reflects the other's needs and aspirations; and they share deeply-felt emotions, ambitions and sensitivities which remain unspoken. They complement each other, like the two faces of a coin. The Tiger brings passion – and the Hare, tenderness – to this relationship.

With THE DRAGON

This is a powerful relationship; and such a couple will have ambition and a driving force which could take them right to the top. The Tiger has a sobering effect on the Dragon, and is able to curb its wilder excesses. But that does not prevent the pair from crossing social barriers. In the worlds of business and entertainment, their magnetic appeal will allow them admittance into the closest of social circles. But they should never let success go to their heads, nor harbour any delusions regarding their own importance. There is an amazing electricity between these two: their love-life will be passionate, exciting and constantly regenerating.

With THE SNAKE

According to Chinese astrological lore, this pairing is sometimes an unhappy one. The Tiger is so exuberant and extrovert, the Snake so darkly mysterious, that they seem to have little in common. At first, mutual attraction hides the cracks in the partnership; but in time, these begin to show. There is a lack of total frankness between them, as if the Snake has some secret that cannot be shared. For the relationship to succeed, openness is essential at all times. Then the partnership will have a chance to blossom.

34

With THE HORSE

Here is someone who shares the Tiger's opinions, aspirations and moral sense, and who admires the Tiger's strength of personality. A devoted admirer, able to give practical and material support, the Horse can be an indispensable companion, who will be at the Tiger's side in times of triumph. The Horse will also be a considerable source of consolation and strength when circumstances are less favourable. With such an ardent and loyal partner, happiness and success is assured. Their love, both in outward displays of admiration, and in more intimate moments, is the envy of many less favoured couples.

With THE SHEEP

The Tiger is inevitably the dominant partner in this relationship. Though they share few interests, it is a happy match. They may be separated for long periods by demands of career or other circumstances, but their moments together will be full of consideration and affection. It does not matter that the Tiger may find the Sheep a little dull and unadventurous at times; this is more than compensated for by the Sheep bringing a gratifying stability to the relationship. Thus, the Sheep looks to the Tiger for romance and excitement, while the Tiger relies on the Sheep for sincerity and companionship.

With THE MONKEY

The Monkey is too much of an individual to be readily won over by the Tiger. The Monkey may even be jealous and resentful of the Tiger's success, remaining cool and aloof, an attitude which the Tiger finds disconcerting. If, however, these two personality types do eventually strike up together, echoes of past incidents may prevent the relationship from developing as deeply as it ought. At first, the Tiger may be amused by the Monkey's flippancy, but it may not be long before the Tiger begins to become weary of the Monkey's casual attitudes to the practicalities of life, even tiring of the relationship itself. The physical side of their love could also be marred by misunderstandings. These, however, can be resolved through patience and consideration.

With THE ROOSTER

This is a glamorous couple, the focus of attention whenever they are seen out together. Both are leaders in their own fields; and the Tiger admires and respects the Rooster's undoubted talents. They have the same addictive zeal and enthusiasm for life; and on the surface, they seem to be exceedingly well-matched. But behind the public mask, the two may be fiercely competitive, revealing an inner insecurity, perhaps due to career anxieties or old-fashioned jealousy. Displays of affection tend to be exaggerated – often to such an extent that they suggest insincerity to the outsider. But such behaviour is characteristic of both zodiacal types, and the Rooster and Tiger are likely to be bound together for life.

With THE DOG

The Dog is a wise choice of partner for the Tiger personality. The Dog shares many of the Tiger's principles, such as honesty, integrity and loyalty. It also admires the Tiger's authoritative manner, while the Tiger takes encouragement from the Dog's quiet but very determined support. Family life is likely to be stable and secure, providing a happy environment for children; and love will be strong and enduring, helping the couple face any difficulties that may arise in their life together. Physical affection plays an important part in the relationship, too, and this is something that will endure right through their lives together.

With THE PIG

Usually, the Tiger finds the Pig a little too mundane to be drawn into a lasting relationship, while the sensible Pig may feel that the Tiger's priorities are altogether wrong. There may be frequent disputes about finances, often arising from the fact that the Pig tends to be the banker in the family, and the Tiger the provider. Given that these are such contrasting types, their love-life may be stormy and unpredictable; and despite the passion, there may be a sense of being left unfulfilled, one partner regretting the lack of old-fashioned romance, and the other a lack of adventure. Much that is left unspoken needs to be said, if this relationship is to have every chance to flourish.

CHAPTER FOUR

THE HARE

Dead embers burst into flame

死灰復燃

Lin gathered up the brushwood, and carried the bundle into the house. Avoiding her eyes, her mother took a few sticks and hurriedly pushed them into the stove. 'You won't be doing this once you are married,' she said, encouragingly. Lin smiled, but her smile was as thin as the spring sunshine.

It was an open secret that negotiations for her betrothal to one of the town's most eligible young men were already under way. Yet she felt strangely empty. She was unable to share her family's elation, and found the obvious envy of her friends far from flattering.

The fire spluttered and smoked. 'Here, let me take that,' said Grandmother. 'These twigs are much too green to burn. And look at those scratches! You want to keep those hands white as lotus-flowers. They should be treated like the hands of a gentlewoman.'

Lin smiled. 'Hardly a gentlewoman, Grandmother. A merchant's wife, maybe. I'll be carrying tack and harness in place of twigs and firewood. There's the difference.' The Widow Lang admonished her daughter with a wagging finger.

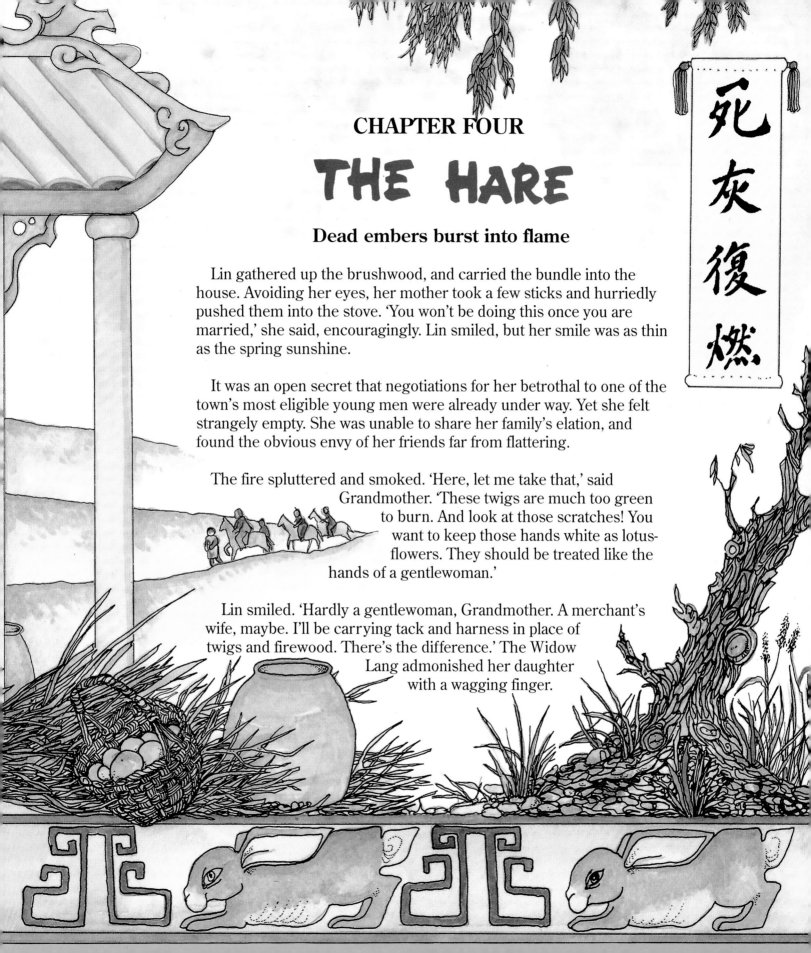

'The difference, my dear, is that tack and harness are bought with gold and silver, while firewood falls off the trees. Now let's get the water boiling for our visitor's tea before they arrive.'

Lin shook her head, enigmatically. Her lack of interest in her imminent betrothal bothered her family. She had accepted the arrangement as a duty. There was not a father who could have wanted a better match for his daughter. Sadly, however, Lin had been without a father for five years, now.

As they spoke, a group of riders, with a couple of attendants on foot, approached. It was Ho Pai, the man who, if everything went well, would soon be Lin's father-in-law. He was no mere merchant, but had all the elegance and grace of a nobleman. It was easy to see from where his son Chang had got his good looks.

Ho Pai dismounted, bowed respectfully to Mrs Lang and greeted her formally. 'My son Chang has asked me to present his compliments to the widow of the respected Mr Lang, and has entrusted me with this trifling gift as a token of his regard for her welfare.'

He handed her a dish covered with a cloth. The Widow gratefully acknowledged it. By the scent, it was preserved ginger. By the weight, there would be a silver tael or two tucked in the covering.

The Widow Lang ushered the merchant into the house, and sat him down, while Grandmother set a jug of rice beer outside for the three attendants. To the Widow Lang's alarm, the smouldering sticks had still not boiled the water for the tea, but happily there was wine to offer her guest.

Lin presented herself without haste or excitement, and poured wine into tiny cups, while her mother and Ho Pai chatted about chrysanthemums, poetry and ornamental fish. Imperceptibly, the conversation soon turned to family relationships, the desirability of marriage, and the eternal worry of finding suitable partners for one's children.

'Here, for example, are the Eight Characters of the birth date for my son Chang. Now where do you suppose I could find a suitable partner for him?'

He handed the Widow Lang a paper, wrapped in a red cover. She received it reverently. The paper, with Chang's name on one side and his birth date on the other, was the traditional way of signalling a formal proposal. Almost a little too readily, Grandmother produced a similar packet.

'We, too, have been wondering what sort of husband is indicated by the Eight Characters of my own daughter. As you can see, she was born in the year of the Hare' said the Widow Lang.

Politely, Ho Pai took the packet.

'More wine for our visitor, my daughter,' cried Grandmother, opening out the red paper, 'while I see what lucky star guides the fortunes of our guest's fine son.'

'I see your son was born in the year of the Horse,' continued Grandmother. 'He will be a great credit to his father.'

'Like father, like son,' laughed Ho Pai.

'And your dear wife? Wasn't she also born in the year of the Horse? I remember that she preferred to ride in the saddle, rather than in a carriage.'

'You are right, venerable lady,' replied the merchant, sadly. 'She was a good woman, but very determined. Perhaps, if she had been less so, she would still be here today.'

Ho Pai suddenly slapped his knees cheerfully. 'Enough of the past. What about the future?'

'And what about your empty wine cup?' asked the Widow Lang, 'Or would you prefer some beer?'

Ho Pai laughed. 'You are a perfect hostess, Madame.'

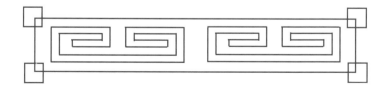

It was not until dusk began to fall that one of Ho Pai's attendants suggested it might be time to leave. At last, the merchant, in a state of satisfaction, was helped slowly to his horse.

The Widow Lang handed one of the attendants a small jar.

'Take this for your master,' she said with a smile. 'And give it to him in the morning. I think Mr Ho will be in need of it.'

The Widow Lang was correct. When, the next morning, Mr Ho felt the need to sample Lin's hangover cure, he was pleasantly surprised by its speedy effectiveness. Over the following days, he found several excuses to dispatch his son to Widow Lang's for various concoctions. This was a discreet way of helping out his future in-laws financially, but it also enabled his son to become better acquainted with the girl he had chosen for him.

'But I don't like her,' Chang told his father.

Ho Pai was stunned. 'How could you not like her? She's a beautiful girl. She's gentle, cultured and would be a great asset to you.'

Chang shrugged his shoulders. 'I can't see her riding off into the hills with me. Can you?'

Frankly, Ho Pai could not. But neither could he see why Chang would want his wife to do so. He had to think long and hard about this. A marriage was for ever. Some said that a couple grow to love each other in time. But was his son's happiness worth the risk, he wondered.

A few days later, Ho Pai made his heavy way back to the Widow Lang's house. Since the proposal had been formally accepted, courtesy – if not the law – demanded that he would have to make some kind of reparation to the family for breach of promise. Fortunately, one of his nephews, like many people born in the year of the Snake, had recently been appointed to a position in the magistrate's office. Ho Pai therefore decided to take him along in case legal advice was needed.

For her part, Lin had been far too dutiful to voice any objection to the arranged marriage. She had no feelings for Chang; she neither liked nor disliked him. Yet the gulf between them was wider than the Eastern Sea.

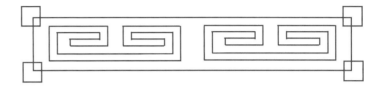

Lin had been setting some gentian to dry by the stove when she saw Ho Pai and the notary arrive. She called to her mother.

'By their slow pace, I would say they were bringing bad news,' said the Widow Lang. Prepare some tea, Lin. I don't think wine will be appropriate today.'

Lin began to tend the stove as her mother went to the door. Ho Pai was visibly ill at ease.

'Widow Lang, I have some very unhappy news. Perhaps it would be best if I let my nephew Ho Ying speak for me.'

Lin threw a few sticks into the stove, and turned to face the visitor. The burning embers blazed into life; and in the copper light of the fire, Lin's eyes caught the young lawyer's face. For a few moments, the flames filled the room with a sudden brilliance. Neither Lin nor the young newcomer moved.

Ho Pai looked quickly at the Widow Lang. She returned his glance, inspiration and understanding passing instantly between the two of them.

'What is this unhappy news you have for me, Mr Ho?' she asked eventually.

Ho Pai took a breath, making a sudden decision.

'Unhappy news? No, no. My voice was not distinct. Happy news is what I said.'

They looked at Lin, and then at Ho Pai's nephew. Smiling, the Widow Lang offered Ho Pai a cup.

'Perhaps a little wine would be appropriate, Mr Ho?'

The Hare personality

While giving the impression that they are shy and retiring, Hare-types are nevertheless very determined people who are able to get what they want through the charm of their personalities. Naturally warm and loving, they make excellent companions. In fact, Hares need to be part of the crowd, where they can feel safe and protected. On a one-to-one basis, too, Hares are able to offer love, and to accept it, but often their affection is misdirected, or not fully appreciated.

Hares frequently conceal their innermost feelings, especially if they believe that their own problems could cause others to be upset. Indeed, in Buddhist lore, the Hare is the symbol of self-sacrifice. Hare personalities are therefore often found looking after children, the under-privileged, animals, the vulnerable and the endangered, and so they make natural nurses, welfare workers and teachers.

Likewise, the Hare is usually a fierce champion of civil rights; and despite the usual association of the Hare with avoidance of confrontation, this personality could be a formidable opponent in a conflict of interests. The Chinese also believe the Hare to be a sharp judge of character, quick to detect insincerity.

A Chinese legend tells of a Hare that lives in the Moon, where it spends its time distilling herbs in order to make the elixir of life. Indeed, those born under the sign of the Hare usually have more than just a passing interest in plants and their many uses, whether culinary or medicinal. Generally, Hares also prefer the gentler arts of reading and writing to any form of physical exertion, though they may be enthusiastic spectators and supporters of a variety of sports.

More so than any other of the animal signs, the Hare's powers of procreation are proverbial. Thus, we would expect the typical Hare personality to have an urgent sex-drive; and in the spring particularly, under the heady influence of lengthening days, the Hare's restraint may not always be as strong as it ought to be.

But it would be wrong to think that the passionate Hare is by nature a fickle creature. Indeed, once the Hare has established a loving relationship, the couple's partnership will be secure and well-founded, even though it may not yet have been formalized by marriage. Care and compassion are central to the Hare's character, and the last thing that any Hare would want to do is to hurt the one it loves.

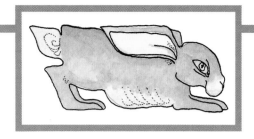

WHO IS THE PERFECT PARTNER FOR THE HARE?

Most people would benefit by having a Hare personality as a partner in life. The Hare's consideration and kindness traditionally provide constant support. However, strongly self-motivated individuals might abuse the Hare's tolerance. Others could find the Hare's gentle insistence extremely irritating – most of all, the flamboyant Dragon, whose good fortune, so the Chinese say, flies away at the approach of a Hare. Nor, it is said, can the Hare expect much attention from the Rooster, who always seems to have more important matters to attend to. But for most signs, Hare personalities provide quiet and reliable companionship, a listening ear, and a helping hand in times of trouble.

If domestic bliss is the criterion, the Hare's ideal companion would be another Hare; the Sheep personality with whom it shares many interests; or the happy, level-headed Pig. But a home-life is not for everyone. So those Hare personalities who want to advance their careers, pursue ambitions, or add a touch of excitement to their lives need the stimulation of someone with more positive, even aggressive, characteristics. The Tiger is the companion sign to the Hare: its objectives are the same as the Hare's, but the approach to life is quite different. A Tiger personality – but only if the Tiger is the male – is not afraid to exhibit those extrovert qualities that the Hare prefers to keep dormant.

Traditionally, however, the Hare's ideal companion is the Snake. Why this should be has never been satisfactorily explained; but observation over the centuries has led the Chinese to say that when the Hare meets the Snake, there is true happiness.

How each of the twelve personality types relates to the Hare

With THE RAT

The Rat personality will be the more dominant partner in this relationship. The two may settle down comfortably, but the Rat is likely to treat the Hare very off-handedly, basically in need of its companionship, but seldom expressing this. Consequently, in this partnership, the Hare is inevitably the loser. This is a relationship that is likely to have been born out of sudden passion, a momentary chemistry drawing the two together. Indeed, were it not for the occasional burst of passion at unexpected moments, the Hare would undoubtedly decide to leave the partnership. Those precious shared moments are well worth waiting for, so it seems.

With THE OX

Here is a partner who is able to offer the Hare much practical support in return for affection. The romance in this partnership is unspoken, but mutual understanding is strong. When there are important matters to deal with, there is rarely any difference of opinion. Both partners tend to be very traditional in their outlook, and if anything is found to be lacking in the relationship, it is a spirit of adventure. It will not harm them if they divert from their set routine from time to time. The love between these two is deep, and physically rewarding, too. The Hare will usually expect the Ox to take the initiative, however.

With THE TIGER

Despite outward differences, this could be the perfect partnership. On the face of it, their interests – and certainly their styles – are incompatible. But, in fact, they only differ in the way they set about achieving what they want. There is a secret understanding between them. If the Hare and Tiger are in business together, or share the same career, they are set to climb to the top. Each is able to fulfil the other's needs, and their love can be both romantic and passionate.

With ANOTHER HARE

There is little amiss with two Hares in partnership. Indeed, if asked what are the essential requirements for happiness, love and affection would be at the top of their list. Strangely, though, loyalty and fidelity might not be regarded as important by either partner, and their bonds are curiously loose. The relationship may be a little too open-ended for most couples, but it is likely to last a lot longer than many conventional partnerships. Both are likely to dote on children, and would love a large family. Home life nearly always takes precedence over career.

With THE DRAGON

The Chinese say that the Dragon's good fortune disappears when it meets the Hare. This is one of the few relationships where the Hare dominates its partner. Attracted by the Dragon personality's amazing charisma, the Hare usually succeeds in ensnaring the object of its affections. Too late, the Dragon partner may discover that there is no way out. Financially or physically, the Dragon may soon begin to weaken, worn out by the Hare's demands on both pocket and affection. If the Hare wants the relationship to last, therefore, it is vital to keep a sense of proportion.

With THE SNAKE

There is something very special about this relationship which defies rational explanation. Love at first sight is a rare dream, but is found in the instant magic which bursts forth when the Snake and Hare first catch each other's eye. If these two meet at the right time, such magic can provide a foundation stone for building the perfect partnership; but if they meet too late, when they have already chosen a partner in life, such ardent fire could destroy what happiness they had before. Snake and Hare often defy convention with a noticeable difference in their ages, especially when the male is the younger partner.

With THE HORSE

Like oil and water, the Hare and Horse may mingle, but never join. Their relationship is one of companionship, rather than love. There is no enmity between them: each partner may care deeply, and honestly, for the other, but they may never know the depths of fulfilment that some other couples experience. Often, such partners do not reveal their innermost feelings until well after middle age, when it is too late to do anything about it. Yet all is not lost, for the advent of a third person into the family relationship – perhaps a child, a relative, or even a rival – frequently acts as the catalyst for future stability and contentment.

With THE SHEEP

The rules of Chinese astrology suggest that the alliance of Hare and Sheep should be highly successful, even though Chinese tradition says that the Hare and the Snake make the best partnership of all. Nevertheless, this is certainly one of the happiest relationships for the Hare, and the only thing that prevents it from being the Hare's ideal relationship is the fact that two such people may be so wrapped up in one another that they forget the realities of the world at large. Though there is no shortage of love, romance or passion here, lack of material comforts in life may put true happiness just out of reach.

With THE MONKEY

The Hare and the Monkey make a most diverting couple. They are far from being well matched, but their differences add spice and novelty to each other's lives. The Hare is always intrigued by the Monkey's continual ability to spring surprises, while the Monkey will be grateful for the Hare's support and consolation when plans go wrong. But life together will not be without its problems: there are many conflicting interests and these will make it difficult for the Monkey and Hare to make decisions. In the end, this could have an unsettling effect on the relationship. When together, Monkey and Hare need to compromise, for the Monkey's teasing sense of fun may sometimes hurt the Hare – perhaps, in extreme cases, physically as well as emotionally.

With THE ROOSTER

This relationship is not one of the easiest for the Hare. Both partners tend to have high expectations of the other. The Hare imagines the Rooster to be some wonderfully gifted genius who can change the world; the Rooster thinks of the Hare as some saintly being, beyond all worldly cares. But when the realization dawns that each is just as human as anyone, the shattered ideal may lead to resentment – especially if either partner feels trapped in an inescapable relationship. Hare and Rooster should avoid making a permanent commitment to each other until they are completely sure that they can cope with the consequences. Inexplicable changes of mood, and a reluctance to enjoy an active sex life, could be due to a misunderstanding of the other's physical needs.

With THE DOG

Initial attraction between the Dog and the Hare may at times be very strong, but an affair built on passion may not last indefinitely. There has to be something more if the relationship is to continue. Unfortunately, the Dog's directness may soon appear abrasive to the fastidious Hare; while the very qualities that originally attracted the Dog to the Hare could eventually pall. Nevertheless, they may well settle down together perfectly happily, providing there is room for them to lead independent lives at times.

With THE PIG

This is one of the happiest relationships for both the Pig and the Hare. When family life is more important than career, and home comforts take precedence over fame and fortune, no two people could settle down more contentedly. In this partnership, the Pig will usually be the provider, making every effort to make the home a haven of affection, warmth, and security; while the Hare, in its turn, will do its utmost to repay the Pig's attention with a great deal of care, kindness and consideration. The comforts of home will always be there, even if the luxuries may be absent – for luxuries are not this pair's most important priority. Nevertheless, there will never be a shortage of the one commodity that money cannot buy – love.

CHAPTER FIVE

THE DRAGON

Retune the string, change the direction

The rain had been falling steadily for three days now. Brooks were swollen into rivers, rivers into torrents, and even the mountain path was awash. A swift-flowing stream had turned the ancient stones, already worn smooth by the feet of generations of pilgrims, into mirrors which glistened in the moonlight, pointing the way to the ruined temple.

Pai-ming struggled upwards, precariously steadying herself on the wet branches of the pine trees, until she finally reached the summit of the hill. The wide courtyard in front of the temple was overgrown with weeds, but the open space was welcome after the darkness of the forest.

From the low wall, she could look down on the lights of the houses in the village below, while behind her loomed the temple. She slipped a bag off her shoulder, and from it took a bronze bowl and a pitcher. Then, pausing to steady her nerves, she carried them to the wall of the temple. When all other remedies had failed, water washed off the roof of a sacred shrine was said to be the final hope of the sick.

Years ago, the eaves of the temple had been elaborately decorated with fantastically carved dragons, but only one of these still survived intact. From its mouth, water spouted.

Pai-ming gathered a bowl of this precious fluid, and was about to pour it into her pitcher, when she noticed that the temple doors, which she thought had been bolted and nailed fast, were ajar. A faint light flickered through the crack. The sudden realization that she might not be alone unnerved her, but curiosity overtook prudence, and she slowly picked her way along the terrace to the temple doors to peer inside.

The light was coming from a single candle, which was enough to illuminate the whole interior. Much to her surprise, the temple appeared to have been recently repaired and renovated. Incense was burning before a statue of T'ai Sui, the God of Time, and thick clouds of perfumed smoke rose to the red-painted roof beams. On either side of the temple hall, rows of wooden statues, decked in red silk robes, stretched far into the distance.

At a desk, a black-robed Taoist priest was studiously writing with a brush.

Pai-ming pushed at the door slightly. To her alarm, it gave a loud creak, alerting the priest. Without looking up, he beckoned her inside, then continued to write. A lightning flash and a crack of thunder set a white owl flapping over her head. Startled, Pai-ming darted in through the doorway.

'It is a late hour to receive visitors.' The priest's hollow voice echoed round the hall. 'Who would trudge through the rain in order to fetch water?'

Cold and wet, Pai-ming was already shivering, but the unexpected meeting was even more chilling. Gathering her courage, she replied: 'The man I am to marry is very ill, and has not opened his eyes for many days. The doctors say he will not survive. That is why I came to collect water from the temple roof.'

The priest continued to write, then said: 'If it is his destiny to recover, he will. All is recorded in the books of the Lords of Time. See there, the sixty ministers of T'ai Sui. One of them has already written your lover's destiny. Do you wish to know it?'

Pai-ming could not speak, but nodded fearfully. The priest took a scroll of paper from a cabinet and studied it carefully. 'Heaven will reward you. Your lover will recover from his illness in three days. You may wash his face every morning with the water you have collected, but you must also give him tea made from the root of the Long Life Flower.

'And now we must see what the Lords of Time have recorded for you. I already know that you were born in the year of the Dragon, for you have special gifts which not all people possess. But beware the Hare; for your powers evaporate like the dew when the Hare approaches. The man who is born in the Year of the Rat can guide you; without his advice, you will come to harm. Choose wisely, or not at all.'

Pai-ming listened apprehensively, troubled by the priest's strange revelations. Then she realized that she had nothing to offer him, either for the rare herbs he had given her, or his prophecy. As if sensing her confusion, the priest held up his hand and said: 'If you wish to show your gratitude, there is something you can do – but not for me.

'Many years ago, I studied at the Monastery of the Red Towers, learning to heal the sick, and to care for the incurable. The monastery is not far from here, but because it was once ravaged by the plague, everyone fears to go there. Those who live there now have all the necessities of life, apart from the joy of meeting people from the world beyond their walls. However, since you are destined to have a long life, you need not be afraid of visiting them. For your offering, therefore, do not take them rice, or fruits, or other such presents. They are not in need of such things. Instead, you must dance and sing for them.'

It was an extraordinary request, and Pai-ming was astonished. Nevertheless, she agreed.

'When I get there, who shall I say sent me?'

The priest paused for a moment, thoughtfully. 'If it is that they still remember me, they will know me as Pu-tso the Taoist.'

Pai-ming followed the priest's instructions carefully, giving Kan the special herbal tea. For three more days, Kan remained in a coma, but on the third morning, as Pai-ming was washing his face, he opened his eyes. And exactly as the priest had foretold, Kan began to make a speedy recovery.

Several weeks passed. The time for Pai-ming's wedding to Kan was approaching; and with each day, her worries mounted.

Sensing her anxiety, Pai-ming's mother tried to reassure her, explaining that it was nothing new for a future bride to have her doubts about leaving home. But Pai-ming had other things on her mind. Until she knew the location of the Monastery of the Red Towers, she was no nearer to keeping her promise to the old priest who had saved Kan's life.

A few of her mother's friends, who had sometimes watched Pai-ming practise dancing, encouraged her to continue, and even persuaded her mother to hire a Music Master to play for her. Unfortunately, Kan came to the house unexpectedly on an errand, found Pai-ming rehearsing with the Music Master, and was furious. Pai-ming felt that it was time to tell him what had happened at the temple.

Although Kan was annoyed, he eventually agreed to a compromise. 'You say you have to keep your promise to that charlatan? Well then, learn your dances. Perform them at the Red Towers monastery, if you will. But from the moment I put my seal to the wedding contract, you will never again dance, neither in public, nor for me – nor for yourself.'

Pai-ming agreed. Later, she spoke to her mother. 'Kan is a year older than I am. If I am a Dragon, what would that make him?'

Her mother looked surprised. 'A Hare. Why?'

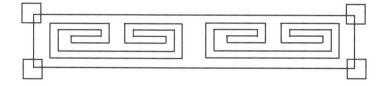

It was the Music Master who discovered the location of the Monastery of the Red Towers. It was not far from the town. Pai-ming, the Music Master, and her mother decided to travel there the next morning. It was an emotional experience. Many of the invalids had not seen anyone from the outside world for many years. The music, and especially Pai-ming's dancing, brought a joy that could only be expressed in tears.

At the close of the display, an elderly nun came to thank Pai-ming and the musicians.

'How fortunate you are to be able to bring so much pleasure to people with your dancing,' said the nun, with sincere gratitude. 'I am sure you will continue to do so for many years. Unfortunately, we have nothing to give you in return, other than our heartfelt blessing.'

Pai-ming gave a wry smile. 'Even that is too much. I am here to repay a debt, and to keep a promise to an old priest who so kindly cured my future husband's illness.'

The nun glanced up at the Music Master.

'I can see why you were so grateful. I know you will be both very happy.'

Confused, Pai-ming felt too embarrassed to correct her, but the nun continued: 'It would be unimaginable that your birth signs were not compatible. What is your animal-year, Miss Pai-ming?' she asked.

'I was born in the Year of the Dragon.'

'And yours, Sir?'

'The Rat.'

Pai-ming's heart began to pound. In her head, she heard the old priest's voice, as loud as it was in the hall of the ancient temple. She had to ask.

'Tell me, reverend lady, do you know an old priest, Pu-tso the Taoist?'

The nun laughed. 'Why, of course I do. He was the founder of this monastery.'

'And when was that?' persisted Pai-ming.

The nun thought carefully for a moment, then replied: 'About six hundred years ago.'

The Dragon personality

You might expect the Dragon sign to be special. After all, it is the only sign of the Chinese zodiac that is an imaginary animal. So it is that in China, the Dragon is regarded as the symbol of authority – well beyond the reach of ordinary mortals, and representing either supernatural forces or the might of the Emperor. Indeed, Chinese families often plan to have their off-spring born in the year of the Dragon, as it is believed that these children, more than any others, will in good time achieve great fame and rise to high office.

Thus, the Dragon-type is frequently found to be the bearer of good fortune, and luck certainly tends to play a large part in the Dragon's attitude to life. Indeed, Dragon personalities are prone to trust to chance, sometimes to the extent of being reckless with their finances, or in their behaviour.

Of all the Chinese astrological types, Dragons are the ones most likely to be gamblers. But, while Dragon-types are destined to have at least one stroke of good fortune in their lives, they sometimes lead themselves into ruin by choosing to rely on chance more than effort. This negative factor often prevents Dragons from achieving the wealth and fame traditionally reserved for them.

The Dragon is a supernatural animal, and magic plays a large part in the lives of those born in the Dragon year – sometimes quite literally, through an interest in the occult and mystic arts. More likely, however, such magic is revealed through the illusory world of the stage, as Dragon personalities are very often active in the performing arts. They revel in the limelight, craving the attention of an adoring public, and are therefore more inclined to be city-dwellers.

Dragon-types are drawn irresistibly to the unusual, bizarre or eccentric. They are great dreamers, and have vivid imaginations, constantly producing speculative plans which may be wholly impractical. Nevertheless, Dragon people have to be admired for an ability to spot the latest trends. They have a flair for fashion, and are apt to set style, rather than to follow it. Even with the minimum of resources, they will never fail to impress with their elegance and remarkable poise.

Constantly on the move, Dragon-types find it difficult to settle, and so are best suited to activities that can be brought to a swift end – ready for the moment when some trivial event sets them off in search of a new adventure.

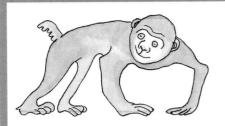

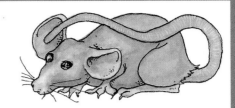

WHO IS THE PERFECT PARTNER FOR THE DRAGON?

It is difficult to resist the attraction of the Dragon personality, and even the most obstinate of the Dragon's critics have to admire its audacity and style. But it is often dangerous to get too close; for although the Dragon may not plan mischief nor deliberately set out to cause harm, there is often a trail of havoc left behind in the Dragon's path. Saddest of all is when the Dragon's closest confidantes see the loved one blindly pursuing some folly which will inevitably lead to ruin.

There are several astrological types who would be ideal companions for the Dragon. Probably the Dragon's preference will be someone like the Monkey or the Rat, eager to play the role of accomplice, and giving encouragement to the Dragon's more untoward plans – even to the extent of providing practical and material assistance. Someone like the Horse or Tiger, will have the opposite effect, helping to curb the Dragon's excesses, while ensuring all that creative energy is put to good use. The Sheep and the Ox would have too much common sense to bother with the Dragon's exotic fantasies.

In love, the Dragon's companion needs to be able to cope with a character who is impulsive and capricious – perhaps even inconstant; so someone like the Dog, who regards fidelity as the most important feature of a relationship, will have none of this. For the Dragon's part, the ideal companion will share the Dragon's zest for life; and as the Dragon craves to be constantly stimulated and aroused by novel experiences, an ideal companion would be someone as reckless as the Monkey, or as scheming as the Rat, who would be eager to accompany the Dragon in its adventures.

How each of the twelve personality types relates to the Dragon

With THE RAT

This is perhaps the best partner for the Dragon, for they will share many ideals and have similar interests. The Rat is able to provide guidance and stimulus for the Dragon's schemes, and can often work out finer details in the Dragon's general plan. The only problem for this couple is that they both excel in thinking up ideas rather than dealing with actual practicalities. But once they put their heads together, they will usually achieve their ambitions. Their love is sincere and enduring. But the Dragon may be a little too openly affectionate for the Rat at times. In private, however, the Rat may be too eager in taking the initiative.

With THE OX

This is not the best of partnerships for the adventurous Dragon. The Ox may be too down-to-earth, while the Dragon's desire to be on the move may be a constant source of dispute. Both have determined ideas when it comes to priorities: but unfortunately, these rarely match, often leading to a lack of direction and a breakdown in communications. Each partner needs to realize that sharing and understanding demand more than just giving in occasionally. Only when the Ox has experienced the Dragon's excitement, and the Dragon has come to terms with realistic living, will these two ever find a happiness which is truly fulfilling.

With THE TIGER

This is a very dramatic, vibrant relationship – the partnership of two strong and ambitious personalities. Although the Tiger may have a dampening effect on the Dragon, the end result is beneficial, for it is only its wilder, more extravagant fancies that are affected by the Tiger's influence. If these two decide to combine personal lives with their careers, they can be a formidable team in business, politics, or the world of entertainment. Certainly, their love-life will be highly charged with a passionate intensity.

With THE HARE

The very vulnerability of the Hare is its great attraction; but according to an old Chinese proverb, when the Hare appears, all the Dragon's luck vanishes. Traditionally, this is one of the least successful partnerships for the Dragon. It will only work if the Dragon is willing to be completely subservient to the Hare, perhaps even going to such extremes as giving up a career. The danger is that, having lost all individuality, the Dragon may also lose the appeal that attracted the Hare in the first place. For this relationship to survive, the Hare must not try to remodel the Dragon's personality.

With ANOTHER DRAGON

Of all the possible partnerships in the Chinese zodiac, the double-Dragon relationship has to be the most unpredictable. Some astrologers would consider this couple to be destined for fame and success, with wealth and honours being heaped on them: others, however, would say it was a recipe for disaster. One thing is certain – this is no ordinary relationship. Such a highly exciting duo has no time for everyday, commonplace matters. They defy traditions to the point of being deliberately shocking, and this may bring trouble in its wake. On an intimate level, too, they will be inclined to be unconventional.

With THE SNAKE

The Snake is the introvert; the Dragon, the extrovert. Such a couple will have a philosophical approach to all problems they encounter in the course of their relationship. Whether discussing global issues or domestic trivia, they will consider every aspect of the situation. The two operate well together, and are able to share many secrets. As lovers, they form a strong attachment, and it is painful for them to be separated for long. The negative side of this is that they can be in danger of losing close contact with former friends.

With THE HORSE

This may not seem to be an ideal partnership at first, but these two outwardly different personalities have much to learn and gain from each other. The Dragon tends to have its head in the clouds; and although there is nothing wrong with imagination and dreams, these can sometimes turn out to be extravagant follies. Without destroying the Dragon's enthusiasm, the Horse is able to add a note of caution, providing constructive and practical criticism when it is most needed. Whether the Horse is the male or female partner, as a lover the Horse is likely to be stronger and more supportive, providing the Dragon with inspiration and encouragement.

With THE SHEEP

Traditionally, Chinese astrologers do not recommend the Dragon and Sheep partnership, since it is a relationship that usually springs from immediate infatuation. The Sheep is impressed by the Dragon's charisma, while the Dragon believes the Sheep to have hidden, unexplored depths. But what the partners see in each other is really a reflection of their own inner selves; and it is all too easy for both to be disillusioned. For the partnership to succeed, the Dragon must realize that the Sheep is a sensitive character who needs constant reassurance of the Dragon's love. Nevertheless, the Dragon must be careful not to stifle romance with excessive passion.

With THE MONKEY

For the Monkey, as well as for the Dragon personality, this is an ideal relationship – but everyone else had better beware, for they are an amazing duo. They form an instant attachment, each able to fulfil the other's basic needs. Never were two minds so closely in harmony, nor two people so prone to create havoc and mayhem, whether accidentally or deliberately. Problems follow these two wherever they go, but only for other people. They themselves are seemingly immune to any kind of disaster. Their love, like other aspects of their lives, is exciting and full of novel experiences; and their affection does not diminish with the passing years.

With THE ROOSTER

If the Dragon is the male partner, this relationship is perhaps as close to the ideal as anything could possibly be. But if the Rooster is the male, then harmony is at risk of being overturned, and the partnership could be blighted by distrust, suspicion and even overt competition. To prevent this happening, both partners should work out agreed guidelines for their relationship, so that each knows what is expected of the other. This not only applies to who is responsible for what in everyday life, but also to their more intimate moments together.

With THE DOG

The Dog and the Dragon are on opposite sides of a Chinese astrological chart. This indicates that the two personalities are so different in character that it is difficult to see how they would ever become attracted to each other in the first place. The Dog, down-to-earth, with a great suspicion of anything unconventional, does not take too readily to the exotic, extrovert Dragon. But it is possible that, having such contrary natures, they are able to recognize and appreciate those very qualities of character they themselves lack. Indeed, if they do become involved emotionally, they may be able to benefit each other by discussing their differing attitudes openly, and sharing their experiences.

With THE PIG

This may not be the best of partnerships for the Pig, who will have to learn to put up with the Dragon's fluctuating moods. The Dragon may depend on the Pig for support, both emotionally and materially, but this can be exhausting for the Pig, if nothing is given back in return. Such a one-way bond of affection can place a great strain on the Pig's tolerance. If this relationship is to survive the ravages of time, the Dragon must be especially considerate towards the Pig, and make a determined effort to return the affection and devotion that is characteristically shown by the long-suffering partner. Then they can be happy together. In romance, the Pig will always be the patient attendant on the Dragon's inclinations.

CHAPTER SIX

THE SNAKE

Too much ceremony hides deceit

Li-hua took the young clerk's hand, and squeezed it gently.
'Are you sure your mother likes me?' he asked, yet again.
'I know it, Pao. She doesn't want to see me married off to some old mandarin. But it's not up to her, is it? Now, in you go.'

Pao tapped nervously on the door, and Li-hua's mother called him in.
'Sit down, Pao,' she said firmly, but kindly. 'I think we're nearly there. But Li-hua's father is going to need a lot more convincing. You know, your employer, Mandarin Chao, has already sent presents.'
Pao grimaced. It was bad enough to have a wealthy rival, but worse when it was the man you depended on for a livelihood.

'Be realistic, young man,' said Li-hua's mother. 'Whatever happens, it will be a few years before you'll be able to look after our little Li-hua properly. That's supposing that Mr Tsang does agree to let her marry you. And suppose we have to sell this place and leave the city. Would you be willing to shut yourself up in the quiet of the countryside with us, Pao?'
Li-hua's mother watched his face carefully.
'I'd do anything for Li-hua, you know that. Anything.'

'What about you, Li-hua?' she called out, perfectly aware that her daughter had her ear pressed to the door. Li-hua came into the room and knelt besides Pao.
'I'd do anything for him, too,' she said.
'That's all I wanted to know,' replied her mother.
'Leave your father to me.'

Mr Tsang heaved his body as he gave a massive sigh, then he shook his head sadly before giving a reply.

'My dear, I know they are in love. And it is right what the sages of old have to say: "When the Snake meets the Hare, there is true happiness." I am sure they are the perfect couple. He seems decent enough to me, and if the circumstances were different, I would be only too pleased to let our Li-hua marry Pao.

'But where will we be if I turn down the Mandarin Chao's proposal? He is very rich indeed, and just think of the business he would be bound to send our way. Could you imagine his reaction if we permitted our daughter to marry his humble clerk? We might just as well pack up and leave the city altogether.'

His wife slapped the table. 'Then let us move! What is more important now? You're not poverty-stricken. You're not seeking civic honours. We could live out our retirement quite comfortably. And with Pao for our son-in-law, who knows how many grandchildren we might have to look after us in our decline! More than we would have if Li-hua marries miserly old Chao, I can tell you!'

Tsang Tsui fanned himself, wearing a look of resignation. 'I know you are right, my dear, but the situation is so difficult.'

Suddenly, Tsang Tsui brightened up.

'Miserly, you called him? That gives me an idea. I must call on my friend, Mr Niu. He knows about these things.'

'What do you want with an antique dealer?' asked his wife. But by the time she had finished her question, Tsang Tsui had already left the house.

Mr Niu put down the vase with the apple-green glaze, and began dusting another, resplendent in reds, blues, and ochres.

'Look at this horrid thing, Tsui. Made to sell in the western lands. No taste at all, those foreign devils. Still, it's a curiosity for someone.'

'Your business is going well, Old Niu?'

'Well enough, Tsui. I had a very good sale recently – an actual letter written by Li Po, the poet, himself. Imagine that!'

'It must have been priceless. Wherever did it come from?'

'You may not believe this, but really, I don't know. It was sent to me anonymously for sale on commission. But so far, no one has come for his share.'

'So you've sold it already?'

'Of course. Almost immediately. Can you guess who bought it?'

Tsang Tsui shook his head.

'Chao the Mandarin. He's a keen collector of literary manuscripts. Is it right he wants to marry your daughter Li-hua?'

Tsang Tsui agreed. 'In fact, that is why I am here. I need your advice. Look, this is his horoscope, which he sent to us as a token of his intentions of marriage to Li-hua. What do you think? Good or bad?'

Old Niu glanced at the card which gave Mandarin Chao's date of birth according to the Chinese calendar. 'I see that our Mandarin friend is a Rat; and your lovely daughter is a Snake. That's easy. Snakes catch Rats. Fine for your daughter, but not so good for Mr Chao the Mandarin.'

Tsang Tsui gave a satisfied smile.

'Thank you, Old Niu. That's just what I wanted to hear. Thank you.'

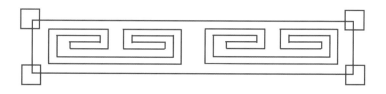

Mr Chao, looking splendid in his robes as Mandarin, Ninth Class with Gold Filigree Button, presided over his guests with all the natural dignity of one who has nobody to oppose him. His principal guests on this occasion were, of course, Tsang Tsui and his family.'

'You do my family a great honour, Mandarin Chao,' said Tsang Tsui, 'but I have to tell you something to your disadvantage. Your horoscope is not, I am afraid, compatible with that of our insignificant daughter. Being born in the year of the Snake, she would bring you ill fortune.'

'Indeed?' replied the Mandarin condescendingly. 'And do you have another suitor in mind? Perhaps you would prefer that she marries my clerk?' The Mandarin paused before continuing: 'Even though he is a thief.'

Although he was seated some way off, Pao heard this and sprang quickly to his feet, protesting his innocence of any crime. The Mandarin waved for silence, then gave a signal to a servant, who came in with a lacquer tray. On it, lay a slim book of manuscripts, bound with silk ribbon.

'This is a volume of the poems of Li Po,' the Mandarin announced. 'A letter, written by the poet, used to be bound with them. However, some time ago it vanished, only to reappear in Mr Niu's shop. I was so anxious to regain the precious document that I immediately bought it back, even though it had been stolen from me.

'I do not know the circumstances by which Mr Niu obtained the letter,' continued Mr Chao, 'but I know that only Pao, my clerk, had access to it. In any case, by dealing in stolen property, Mr Niu is just as guilty as the thief. But this is a time for celebration, so I should be generous. The letter is safe, and in view of my great joy at the prospect of marriage to Tsang Li-hua, I am inclined to forget the whole unpleasant incident.'

'With respect, Mandarin Chao,' said Li-hua, 'how is it possible for you to prove that the letter was originally yours?'

The Mandarin smiled triumphantly, as if it was the very question he had been waiting for.

'You can see for yourself. The holes in the side of the letter exactly match the holes in the binding.'

Li-hua still did not sound convinced. 'Mandarin Chao, would you permit me to assure myself that this is indeed your letter, and untie the ribbon so that I may compare the positioning of the holes more closely.'

Frostily, the Mandarin agreed.

The guests watched fascinated as Li-hua carefully positioned the treasured letter over the book of poems.

She scrutinised them carefully, then announced: 'A perfect match.'

The Mandarin smiled effusively. 'Now perhaps you have learnt to accept the word of a Mandarin.'

'Pao is not a liar, nor is he a thief,' cautioned Li-hua. 'As to the matter of the letter, fortunately there is a witness here to tell us exactly what happened.'

Most of the guests stared blankly at her, but Li-hua's father caught a familiar, enigmatic look in his daughter's eye.

'You see, this ribbon is quite old. It easily shows up any creases, and you can see that there are six, where the ribbon has been folded through the lace-holes in the cover.

'The ribbon is the only witness to what really happened. The holes in the letter could have been made deliberately, simply by placing the letter under the book, and marking the positions of the lace-holes with a sharp point. But unless this were done expertly, the fragile ribbon would also get punctured as the needle was pushed through.

'However, it was not done expertly enough. My eyes are keen, and if I hold this ribbon to a lamp, I can see the tiny marks where the needle pierced the ribbon just at the sides of the creases. Now why should that be, I wonder?'

The Mandarin stared ahead, impassively.

Li-hua turned to Old Niu. 'I hope you got a good price for your letter, Mr Niu. Somehow I don't think the seller will be calling to collect his share of the proceeds.'

She held her hand out to Pao, and with a graceful bow to the Mandarin, led the guests to the door.

The Snake personality

In Chinese astrology, the Snake has a strong, positive image – whereas, in the West it is often associated with evil. Snake personalities are renowned for their grace and elegance. In fashion, they have classic good taste, and show restraint without ever appearing dowdy. They are, in the main, refined, cultured people, who have the ability to be respected without needing to be popular as well. Their opinion will always be consulted, and few changes will be seen to take place without the Snake's approval.

Snake-types could not be accurately described as born leaders, but they may rise to the top of their career or social class with minimal effort. Snakes certainly know how to get on in the world, somehow always managing to be in a situation that brings them into contact with those who really matter. For many Snake personalities, the best example of this is the ability to make a good marriage.

Snakes, in addition, have an uncanny knack of discovering secrets, but this is coupled with an admirable reluctance to divulge the information. Indeed, the more embarrassing, or the more salacious, the secrets are, the less chance there is of keeping them from the Snake's prying nature.

The positive side of this is the Snake's investigative abilities, which can be put to good use in careers that involve research, detection or espionage. Unfortunately, however, the Snake may sometimes put these talents to the wrong use, and thereby gain a reputation for being rather meddlesome and a gossip.

But perhaps the Snake personality's greatest failing is the age-old problem of jealousy. This is not simply a case of being over-possessive: the fault lies much deeper. Ever watchful, ever mistrustful, the Snake needs constant reassurance that the partner is being faithful. Such self-doubt and lack of confidence may stem from an incident that occurred early in life, when the Snake felt betrayed. But this fear must be conquered, for jealousy can be a destroyer.

Yet strangely, it is the partner who should be the jealous one, for the Snake has a reputation of being a seducer. Certainly, the hypnotic charms of the Snake – whether male or female – can be a fatal attraction for any who fall under the spell, since the sensuous signals that the Snake sends out are often misinterpreted. The Snake also sometimes adopts a high moral tone, which can only too easily confuse an ardent admirer.

WHO IS THE PERFECT PARTNER FOR THE SNAKE?

Chinese tradition claims that when the Hare meets the Snake, there is perfect happiness. Astrologers poring over their charts might agree – but perhaps only half-heartedly; for while Hare and Snake are not incompatible, there are more ideally-suited companions for the Snake to choose. Perhaps two people being totally in love is not quite the same as having the ideal partner: after all, love is sometimes the recipe for disaster.

The most compatible signs for the Snake would be the Ox or the Rooster. But though either of these partnerships may be successful, the style of relationship would be quite different. The Ox would provide the practical and physical means to carry out the Snake's cleverly thought-out plans. The Snake and Rooster partnership, however, would achieve quite different results, since both tend to be fond of anything that is unusual.

An even more exotic and adventurous companion for the Snake might be the Dragon; but in this relationship, the Snake is likely to play second-in-command.

It will be important for the Snake to have a partner who can understand his or her physical needs. Fantasy and role-playing also play an important part in the Snake's romantic activity. The down-to-earth Ox, especially, may find this aspect of the partnership difficult at first. Snakes, too, are avid diarists, keeping a record of all their experiences and thoughts, both before and after finding companions in life. Casual acquaintances, therefore, need to bear this in mind.

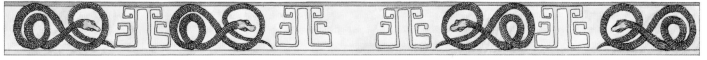

How each of the twelve personality types relates to the Snake

With THE RAT

This is a very one-sided relationship, with the Snake being the dominant partner. Although this situation may suit the Snake, it can often lead to unspoken resentment on the part of the Rat, which is likely to erupt suddenly, leaving the Snake alone and totally vulnerable. It would therefore be in the Snake's best interests to make sure that the Rat partner has no hidden grievances. The best way of doing this is to have honest discussions, during which all issues relating to the relationship can be brought into the open. Because the physical and emotional needs of this couple are worlds apart, they also need to pay particular attention to each other's body language.

With THE OX

In this relationship, the Ox will be a very supportive partner, even if the Snake is found to be rather less stable emotionally; while the Snake will be able to assist the Ox in ways that are less obvious, but just as important. Both partners will be willing to make sacrifices to ensure that the relationship continues since it obviously provides most of what each needs. Their love combines two strongly contrasting approaches, yet it is mutually fulfilling.

With THE TIGER

It is worth considering the factors that draw Tiger and Snake together. Certainly, both types have distinct attractions – the Tiger, physical magnetism, and the Snake, emotional charm. But in romantic matters, the Tiger tends to prefer frank discussion, while the Snake considers that certain topics are best left alone. In some ways, the female Snake has very old-fashioned attitudes towards romance, preferring chivalrous and gentlemanly qualities in the partner. This can appeal to the Tiger who is eager to make a good impression. But once the relationship has taken root, the Snake may find it necessary to endure some rougher habits.

With THE HARE

Chinese astrology considers this to be the most favourable of all the relationships in the zodiac. And, according to tradition, it is the one most likely to result from love at first sight. The only danger that could possibly arise ultimately to threaten the relationship is that these two people may fall so much in love that they neglect careers or family responsibilities. As there could be many children from the marriage, it is essential to maintain discipline in the family from the start. Nevertheless, strictness in the home is bound to be balanced by much love and warmth.

With THE DRAGON

In this emotionally and physically stimulating relationship, both Dragon and Snake instinctively respond to each other's psychological needs. Their love can be intense, making separation – for reasons of work, for example – very painful. Together, they make a fiery partnership, which can be a source of amazement to those whose relationships are far more routine and unremarkable. Those individuals who believe they have something to gain by tangling with this powerful pair need to beware the consequences. The Dragon and Snake are very protective of each other, and do not welcome interference.

With ANOTHER SNAKE

In this mutual admiration society, each will see the partner as an embodiment of his or her own virtues; and while modesty prevents them from blowing their own trumpets, the one never fails to find an opportunity to praise the accomplishments of the other. These two can live in close and perfect harmony – planning, plotting and working together. Their physical love is exploratory and fulfilling, and is destined to remain rewarding for a long time. Snakes will often have similar interests and hobbies, and these undoubtedly add to their intellectual compatibility.

58

With THE HORSE

While the Snake and the Horse may have different interests, and even seem poorly matched, the relationship is probably safe enough to allow both to get on with their own lives without interference. If the Snake partner is female, and happy to accept a traditional role, she can be sure of a supportive and generous partner. But for a male Snake personality, there is the danger that a female Horse partner could become too self-assured, taking many aspects of the relationship for granted. The Snake will gradually come to understand how important an established circle of friends is to the Horse, but that these friends will usually be of the same sex, so that there is little danger of dalliance.

With THE SHEEP

Although not the ideal relationship for the Snake, there is no shortage of love and commitment. They have many shared interests, including their taste in music and literature, which may have first drawn them together. Neither wants to be the dominant figure, and each is happy to look after the other's needs. There is often more romance than might be expected. The Snake needs to come to understand the fastidiousness of the Sheep, and must be wary of taking advantage of the partner's frequent self-sacrifice. The Sheep, however, will need to be more tolerant of the Snake's concern with getting to the top and intense sense of competition outside the family circle.

With THE MONKEY

The magnetic charisma of both Monkey and Snake probably drew these two unalike types together in the first place. But this is sometimes an unsafe relationship, since it may be difficult to steer it through troubled waters, or break it off when things begin to go wrong, for the two are mysteriously linked. Both should enjoy the magic while it lasts, but neither should examine it too closely or the illusion may be shattered. The physical side of the relationship is likely to be a strong factor in keeping the couple together. The Snake needs to come to appreciate that the Monkey needs constant praise and encouragement.

With THE ROOSTER

Although, according to Chinese folklore, the Snake and the Rooster are often at odds, this could be one of the more successful relationships for the Snake personality – particularly if it is closely tied up with career and business. The Rooster has a special kind of flair which the Snake finds highly stimulating. Provided that the Snake makes allowances for the Rooster's assertiveness and tremendous self-pride – and the Rooster appreciates that the Snake usually requires a gentle push in order to achieve fulfilment in life – this partnership should thrive. As this couple matures together, so the relationship develops and flourishes. In times of trouble, the Rooster will be characteristically loyal and supportive.

With THE DOG

There are few points of contact for the couple in this relationship, as their worlds – including attitudes and opinions formed in early childhood – may be too far apart for them ever to establish real harmony. The Dog is considerably more conservative than the Snake as a rule, while the Snake is often on a rather different intellectual plane and tends to have the upper hand. Nevertheless, if the two are drawn together and form a long-term relationship, the Snake should benefit from having a Dog as a supportive and faithful partner, though there may be several misunderstandings that severely test the Dog's loyalty.

With THE PIG

In this relationship the Snake tends to dominate, but this is not something the Snake should consider an advantage. Indeed, it may become aggravating for both parties. Something is lacking when a partner is regarded as the opposition, rather than a companion who offers constant support. Great effort must be put into the relationship in order to keep it alive. Both types have the capability to make the partnership work; but unless there is some other factor – perhaps a shared career, or even children – to give this couple an objective, the two could be in danger of drifting apart from time to time. They will need to work hard at achieving mutual understanding.

CHAPTER SEVEN
THE HORSE

Who's the man and who's the woman?

'Hurry with the duck's feet! Two more fried bean curd! And I'm still waiting for another basket of date dumplings.'

With a few deft movements, the cook swept the scalding food from the iron pans on to the plates. Her daughter, Mo-lan, dashed outside and, just as expertly, slid the dishes on to the tables.

Grateful for the shade of the raffia mats above their heads, customers packed the covered yard of the little inn. For Mo-lan and her mother, the longest day of the year was also the busiest. People from all over the province had gathered at the horse-market to watch or take part in the annual sporting contests. Although there was always great interest in the archery and wrestling, nothing attracted such crowds, nor such high stakes, as the horse events. During the next five days, honours and fortunes would be won and lost.

The inn's customers were mostly strangers, though there were a few local lads at a corner table. Those not yet drafted by Mo-lan to help out at the inn were looking forward to showing off their skills, and perhaps winning a trophy or two, later in the day.

One of the lads called out to the kitchen: 'Hey, Mo-lan, how fresh is the dried fish?'

'Fresh today. Just like the wine!' she shouted, above the din. The young men guffawed loudly at the old joke.

There was no doubting Mo-lan's popularity with the boys; her looks and personality were envied by all the girls for several miles around. But they respected her because it was common knowledge that she had eyes only for one.

'Come on, boys!' cried one of the hands. 'Eat up, drink up, and pay up! Or the horses will wonder where we are.'

In the best of spirits, the youths set to work on their rice bowls, and cleared them in minutes. As they were finishing, another man approached. Older than the young hopefuls at the table, he had an air of self-assurance and authority. His shirt was soaked with sweat, and his face wore the triumphant expression of one who has just gained a first prize. One of the lads whistled.

'Hey, Mo-lan, look sharp. Your lover's here.'
Kung grinned, and spread a piece of paper out on the table. The youths stared at it in wonder. It was an imperial currency note.

Mo-lan saw it, too, but feigned disinterest.
'So that's what you call money, is it, Kung? Does that mean you're going to marry me at last?'
Kung shrugged his shoulders, pretending disdain, but he was inwardly embarrassed.
'There's the chance you've been waiting for, Kung. Go on, ask her,' urged Pai-hu.
'I would never marry a woman who proposed to me,' he said haughtily. 'I have my pride.'

'But I've got real money, Kung,' retorted Mo-lan, setting a pitcher of beer in front of him. 'You can take my offer or leave it. You'll not get a better one round here.' She was right, and they both knew it.

Kung gulped down his beer. He hated women who chased after him, and there were certainly plenty of them. There was no denying that Mo-lan was as good a catch as ever there was. But it was the man's job to catch the woman – not the other way round. The trouble was that Mo-lan was too forward. A Fire-Horse, his mother had said; too wilful for a wife. It would need a Tiger to tame her, she said. And he was that Tiger.

Kung emptied the pitcher of beer, and stood up.
'I'm going back to the races. Someone's got to show them what real men are like.'
'Real men?' scoffed Mo-lan. 'You? Sitting on a donkey and thinking you're Genghis Khan?'
'You think it's easy riding a horse?' Kung answered. 'You should try it!'

'Oh, you men are so vain. Anything a man can do, a woman can do better.'
'Is that so?' cried Kung, nettled. 'I suppose you fancy your chances in a race, then?'
'Why not? What are the stakes?'
Kung held up his prize money. 'If you're so keen, what about this, Mo-lan?'
'Why not?' she replied, with a strange look in her eye. There was a buzz of excitement. The loyalties of the local lads were divided between Mo-lan and their hero, Kung. Some tried to dissuade her from being so rash, but she stood firm. Her mother looked askance, and even Kung was forced to ask Mo-lan: 'Presumably, you can ride a horse?'

Mo-lan raised her eyebrows. 'Presumably, I can.'
Kung was perplexed. She could have been bluffing, but he had learnt long ago not to be surprised at any of Mo-lan's talents.
'Right. Where and when?' asked Kung.
Mo-lan glanced at the packed yard of the inn. Every eye was on her. Even the other customers had become caught up in the dispute, and the prospect of a novel – and spontaneous – race eclipsed all the official sporting events. 'Here and now,' Mo-lan answered.
Her mother threw her hands up in despair. Kung sent for horses while the course was decided on.

Several bystanders set themselves up as course-markers, judges, and even bookmakers. Word travelled fast, and by the time Mo-lan, Kung, and their horses were ready, a large, excited crowd had lined the make-shift racetrack. The signal was given, and the two riders charged forward.

Very soon, Mo-lan was ahead. As they reached an old tree, which marked the halfway point of the course, Kung began to overtake her; it almost seemed as if she was pulling back. He now rapidly overtook her and soon galloped past the inn.

Strangely enough, Mo-lan herself did not seem at all concerned about losing. The race had been exhilarating, and her face shone with excitement. Glumly, her mother came out with enough copper cash to cover Kung's prize money. The young man wiped his face, and with genuine admiration commiserated with Mo-lan.

'Oh, that was nothing. Just a canter. Now, I'm in the mood for a proper race.'

'What do you mean, a proper race?'

'If you're up to it, a longer course, and higher stakes.'

'You mean, twice the distance?' Kung looked at the money on the table. 'And twice the stakes?'

'Oh, much more than that,' said Mo-lan scornfully. 'I'll stake my half share in the inn.'

Kung faltered. His most valuable possession was his horse; but even that was worth only a fraction of what Mo-lan was proposing. The cash prize and currency note shrivelled into insignificance. He couldn't possibly match Mo-lan's wager. But Mo-lan had an answer ready for him.

'And if I win, I claim you for my husband.'

The onlookers gasped, and then applauded.

Hearing the commotion, the bystanders who had drifted away after the finish of the last race now hurried back, bringing many more excited spectators with them.

Pai-hu took Kung to one side. 'Listen, this could be an honourable way of marrying Mo-lan. Just be sure to lose the race.'

Kung stared at the youth, glassily.

'I didn't hear you. What did you say?' Kung growled.

Pai-hu shook his head, and walked away.

With a look of mock seriousness, the steward took a pennant from his gown, unfurled it with ceremony, and gave the signal for the race to begin. Taken by surprise, both Mo-lan and Kung made a bad start, but Kung recovered first, and was speeding towards the tree that marked the first turn in the course before Mo-lan even had her horse under complete control.

Mo-lan frantically urged her horse on, and soon she was almost level with Kung. On and on they galloped, to the shouts and cheers of the crowd. Mo-lan pressed forward, screaming to her horse, inching forward, and gaining slowly and painfully. Then, suddenly, it was over. Kung had won. Mo-lan wept with bitter disappointment and frustration. Kung held up a beaker of wine, flushed with success and pride.

'To an honourable loser,' he cried. He turned to Mo-lan, but she had her back to him, her face buried in her hands. She had lost everything, and for what? Kung felt a great surge of pity well up inside him. He knew what he had to do.

'As the winner of this race,' he cried, with stern authority, 'I claim my rightful prize. Mo-lan, I demand that you be my wife.'

Mo-lan turned round, scarcely believing what she heard. Slowly, she stood up, and then, to a roar from the delighted crowd, threw herself into Kung's arms.

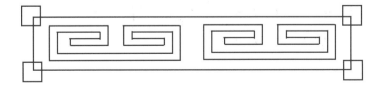

The Horse personality

Whenever the issue of equal rights for men and women arises, you can be sure that one of the most vociferous speakers will be the Horse personality – for the sign of the Horse is intimately concerned with gender, and the separate roles that men and women play.

The Chinese identify everything in terms of yin – the feminine, receptive side of nature, identified with the Moon – and yang, the masculine, positive side, represented by the Sun. When the Buddhist monks of old decided to give animal names to the twelve signs, they chose the Horse to symbolize the yang force at its most intense. In the Chinese calendar, the Horse month includes the longest day; and the Horse hour is from noon, when the Sun is at its highest point. In those ancient times, a fine horse was as much a status symbol as a fast car or motorbike for young men today.

The typical man born in the year of the Horse holds traditional views, and enjoys the fellowship of his companions in clubs and societies. He likes to take part in sports and team activities, but may be unwilling to participate as an individual: recognition as a member of a group is far more important than personal honour.

For the female born in a Horse year, however, this basic characteristic may become a constant source of contention: for if she is not accepted by men as an equal, she may withdraw into herself entirely, and find consolation in the companionship of her own sex. It may then be very difficult for her to establish relationships with men.

No astrological type has such strongly formed misconceptions about the roles of the sexes, whether in everyday life, or in a one-to-one relationship. Both male and female Horse-types therefore need to try to understand the role of the opposite sex more sympathetically.

Alone among all the signs of the Chinese zodiac, tradition singles out a certain Horse-type for special mention. It is said that the Fire Horse year – the most recent was 1966 – breeds tyrants and despots, and that Fire Horse children become a generation of revolutionaries, Fire Horse women being regarded with particular awe. Indeed, so great was the fear of Fire Horse girl children, and the difficulty in finding husbands for them among the ancient Chinese, that infant mortality was always much greater in years of the Fire Horse.

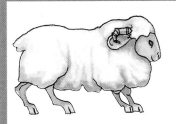

WHO IS THE PERFECT PARTNER FOR THE HORSE?

The Horse personality can be very difficult to live with; and unfortunately, not everyone whom the Horse regards as a convivial companion returns affection. It is therefore not so much a question of finding the right partner for the Horse – who assumes that everyone is a friend until proved otherwise – as finding someone for whom the Horse is the right partner. Horse-types, of course, would themselves have much in common, although two Horse partners may find they are too similar to be stimulating company for long. However, the Sheep personality – the companion sign to the Horse – could prove to be a dependable and supportive partner.

Other zodiac types who are most likely to feel comfortable in the company of the Horse are the loyal Dog, and the authoritative, dynamic Tiger. As friends, these three form a powerful, close-knit team, whether as a family group, or in some business enterprise. Indeed, the ideal family unit for the Horse is created when the partner is either the Dog or the Tiger, and their first child belongs to the third sign of the trio. Such a family will have great confidence in itself, the bonds of affection between family members will be very strong, and the family may even achieve honour and become wealthy.

But for a more light-hearted romance, if the time is not yet appropriate for long-term commitment, the Horse will find the exotic charms of the Dragon personality very attractive, while the witty and entertaining Monkey will constantly amuse. After a while, the Horse personality may find that friendly dalliance with either of these partners finally matures and develops into something more serious and lasting.

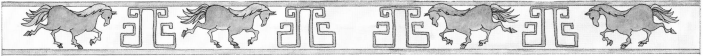

65

How each of the twelve personality types relates to the Horse

With THE RAT

Although the Horse and the Rat are very contrasting types, it is not uncommon for them to form a strong partnership. Unfortunately, however, their roles are not always supportive, especially when both are attempting to get as much out of the relationship as possible. As a result, the Horse may eventually consider this partnership unsatisfactory. If the Rat is the older partner, the Horse may be intimidated and the relationship may become weakened. But if the Rat is the younger partner, the Horse may become demanding and overbearing. This relationship works better when both partners are more mature.

With THE OX

There is often an immediate attraction between the Horse and the Ox, but differences of style soon drive a wedge between them. The Horse may find the Ox too limited in experience, or not adventurous enough, to keep the spark between them alight. The Horse may also resent the way the Ox keeps objecting to the Horse's old friends and life-style. There is a danger that, for the Horse, boredom could soon reveal cracks in this relationship. But all is not lost: if children are born early in the marriage, they should provide a focus of attention that will bind the family together.

With THE TIGER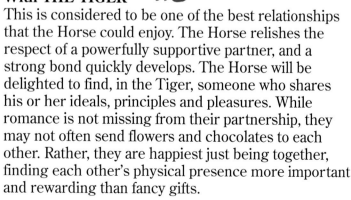

This is considered to be one of the best relationships that the Horse could enjoy. The Horse relishes the respect of a powerfully supportive partner, and a strong bond quickly develops. The Horse will be delighted to find, in the Tiger, someone who shares his or her ideals, principles and pleasures. While romance is not missing from their partnership, they may not often send flowers and chocolates to each other. Rather, they are happiest just being together, finding each other's physical presence more important and rewarding than fancy gifts.

With THE HARE

The physical enjoyment of love is central to the psychological well-being of both the Hare and the Horse; but, strangely, there is something missing from this relationship – the romantic expression of their innermost feelings. Often, both types feel embarrassed about putting their affections into words. When things go wrong, and the partnership teeters, it is also very difficult to repair it. Both find themselves in an awkward position, afraid of being rejected, and often too cautious to make the first move. But events outside the relationship can often trigger a response which will drive them straight back again into each other's arms.

With THE DRAGON

It will not take long for the Horse to be drawn to the Dragon's exciting personality and life-style. The Dragon makes an immediate impression, but it takes a little longer for the Horse to be accepted by this exotic and independent character. Nevertheless, if the Horse is patient enough, and knows how to win the Dragon over, there is ample scope here for a really sympathetic relationship. Their love will deepen as mutual understanding grows, with the Dragon leading the Horse to stimulating new experiences, and constantly rekindling the Horse's spirit of adventure.

With THE SNAKE

The Horse may be fascinated by the Snake's elegance and charm, but there is no guarantee the Snake will respond. However, if the Snake is vulnerable and needs help, the strength and support of the Horse as a friend and companion will be appreciated. It is difficult to see, though, what the Snake may be able to offer in return, unless the Horse considers the Snake's company to be ample reward in itself. Once they have made clear the differences in their likes and dislikes, in everyday life as well as in a physical relationship, they have every chance of surviving the test of time.

With ANOTHER HORSE

Two Horse partners may well have known each other from childhood, or at least from college days. Indeed, they may have known each other long before their friendship eventually developed into something more intimate. Certainly, they have a lot in common – not just their recreational interests, but also attitudes to life, opinions on social issues, and everyday domestic matters as well. But when it comes to the battle of the sexes, ideas about the man's role in life, and that of the woman, may lead them quite frequently into heated discussion.

With THE SHEEP

These two companions should be ideally suited: for although they share many interests, there are still enough differences between them to make their personalities that bit more attractive to a partner. Indeed, the Horse-Sheep relationship is the very model of the traditional family unit, and works best when the male partner, the Horse, is the breadwinner, with the Sheep being content to take the traditional supporting role as home-maker. When the Horse is female, all is not lost, however, but she inevitably becomes the active, dominant partner, taking the lead and making decisions not only in their domestic life but also when it comes to romance.

With THE MONKEY

It is said that the Chinese used to put a monkey in a horse's stable in order to keep it amused. This may have been sound psychology, since they discovered that the horse was generally much fitter and more contented as a result of having to cope with the monkey's presence. So, perhaps not surprisingly, the Chinese also believe that someone born in the Monkey year is one of the best companions for the Horse personality. The two relate well to each other, the Monkey companion generally proving to be a constant source of stimulation and delight for the Horse personality. For a couple whose business and domestic interests are not linked, and for whom a happy and contented home life is more important than honour and riches, this partnership could be ideal.

With THE ROOSTER

There could be problems in this relationship. This is because both partners like to lead independent lives, so much so that they may not relish the idea of surrendering themselves to a partner completely. Here are two people who prefer to retain their individual identities. But, of course, if they have drawn up precise guidelines as to how they are going to run their lives together, there should be fewer difficulties. What should be borne in mind, however, is that the Horse personality may eventually grow to resent the Rooster's more flamboyant life-style. Romance may be in short supply, but not physical passion.

With THE DOG

Chinese astrologers traditionally regard this partnership as a highly successful one for a couple whose domestic life is tied to business or career commitments. But even if this is not the case, this is still one of the strongest bonds that the Horse personality can possibly make. The Dog will prove to be faithful to its life companion; and even though usually the younger partner, will be actively supportive of the Horse in times of trouble and stress. Mutual attachment is evident whenever they are seen together. As a result of such confidence in one another, the home is bound to be a happy one.

With THE PIG

The Horse and Pig often seem to have drifted together. Ask them when they first met and each is likely to give a different answer. The chances are that it was not during the most memorable time in their lives. Their bonding probably began much later; and while friends could see them drawing closer together, the two personality types would probably have been the last to realize that their names had been linked romantically. The Pig, either as the male or female partner, will always be supportive to the Horse, and make sure they both have a comfortable home. As for their love life, it will tend to feature a touch of passion, a dash of romance, a modicum of companionship, and considerable affection – all of these qualities combining to make them a happy and contented partnership.

CHAPTER EIGHT
THE SHEEP

A broken mirror is restored

Silently, the boat turned a bend in the river, and sailed out of the ravine into a broad, open valley. Its dozen or so passengers began to collect their belongings, ready to hurry from the little craft the moment it tied up at the jetty. The old helmsman smiled toothily at a young woman travelling alone, and – in response to her question – pointed ahead. With mixed feelings of wonder and apprehension, Yen had her first glimpse of the dazzling golden roofs of the lamasery of the Orpiment Buddha.

She clambered off the boat, and pushed her way though the crowd of pedlars and villagers that had gathered on the river bank. The lamasery was still a long way off, but at least it was in sight. She followed a dusty cart track that led away from the river, and soon left the bustling riverside village behind.

After walking several miles, Yen began to tire. The lamasery still seemed as far away as ever, and so she decided to rest. She sat down, and from her small bundle of possessions took a morsel of rice-cake, which she slowly began to chew. After a while, she closed her eyes, lulled to sleep by the gentle tinkling of sheep bells, and the faint, plangent tones of a shepherd's pipe.

After a while, Yen woke with a start. The sheep bells were louder now, though their music was drowned by the strident cawing of white-throated rooks. As Yen opened her eyes, she was alarmed to see a young man who seemed to be watching her. He was tanned by the mountain sun; his hair was long and unkempt; and he wore a primitive, hide jerkin which he had most probably made himself.

Seeing that Yen was awake, he held out to her a piece of peach on the point of a knife. She took it gratefully, wondering if the mountain folk spoke the same language as city people. She was pleased to find that they did.

'You must be going to the lamasery,' he said. When she nodded in reply, he added: 'I can come with you. I have to take the sheep to higher ground before the summer is over.'

The stranger gazed at her intently, but his stare was neither rude nor discomforting.

'There aren't many pilgrims this time of the year. You're late for the festival.'

'I'm not a pilgrim,' Yen corrected him. 'I'm going to be a nun.'

The shepherd appeared shocked. 'But you're too young. Nuns are old women.'

Yen laughed. 'They must have been young once.'

'I don't think you should be a nun at all. Just do what all the pilgrims do. Go to the lamasery, pray to the Buddha, and get the High Lama's blessing.'

The shepherd seemed genuinely concerned for her, but Yen just shook her head. 'It isn't as easy as that,' she replied, gathering up her bundle.

'Wait,' cried the shepherd. 'I must come with you. The path gets very steep and dangerous later on, but there's a refuge where most pilgrims stay overnight. Then you can finish the last part of the journey.'

Though she still had doubts about accepting his offer to act as her guide, she was grateful for the company. It was a long and lonely journey to the mountain retreat, and she had been disappointed – and a little uneasy – about travelling alone.

The shepherd gathered his provisions into a pack. Yen watched as he fastened it on to his back with hessian straps. It pulled him up straight and made him look so much taller, and more commanding. He strode off with a determined step. Yen picked up her bundle and – not without some misgivings – followed him obediently.

The sun had already set by the time the shepherd and Yen reached the refuge. It was a crude stone hut, affording only the most primitive shelter.

'Tell me,' he asked, as they sat watching the fire, 'what made you want to become a nun? Wouldn't you rather marry?'

Yen's face clouded over. 'I was going to marry, but cannot. I am under an obligation to enter the lamasery. You see, until last year, I was engaged to a young man from my town. He was from a good family, and my parents sought the advice of an astrologer. He said that as I was born in the year of the Sheep, and the young man in the year of the Pig, we would be greatly in love. He said we would even be prepared to sacrifice our lives for each other.'

The shepherd stoked the fire and stirred the pot. 'So, you're a Sheep, then? I'm a Dog – a dog looking after sheep – like you, perhaps.'

He turned to her and grinned. 'So the astrologer was wrong?'

'No. His prediction came true, unhappily so. The man I was supposed to marry was called Chu-hsin. We fell in love as soon as we were introduced. Every day, he wrote me beautiful letters, and we counted the hours to the time when we would be married.

'Then, a terrible thing happened. There had been rumours of a plot to overthrow the Emperor, and a high official in our town was accused of being a rebel. Several people in the city were arrested and executed, and one of them was a Mandarin who knew Chu-hsin's father. Because of that, Chu-hsin's father was accused of treason as well, and the whole family was thrown into prison.

'When I heard the news, I ran to the tribunal to plead for Chu-hsin's family, and swore that they were loyal to the Emperor. I even offered myself as hostage in their place. The investigator listened sympathetically, and asked me if I would be willing to stake my life on their innocence. When I agreed, he proposed to drop all the accusations against Chu-hsin's family, provided that I renounce the worldly life, and pray continually for the well-being of the Emperor for the rest of my days.'

Yen looked down, but tears had already begun to form. Quietly, the shepherd passed her a bowl of the broth he had just boiled.

'So that is why I am travelling to the lamasery. Tonight may be last I ever spend outside its walls.' The shepherd said nothing. Yen lay on the blanket that he had spread out for her, and rested her head on the bundle. She closed her eyes, but found it difficult to sleep. The close presence of the shepherd, and his strange silence, disturbed her. It was both comforting and threatening.

The shepherd leant over her and whispered softly: 'Yen, listen to me. Tomorrow you will be shut up away forever. You will never know the pleasures of being with a man. Don't leave the world behind without being fulfilled.'

He reached out, and closed his arms around her shoulders.

The touch terrified her, and she shuddered in horror. With a scream, she pushed the shepherd away, and ran from the refuge, stumbling over stones, and cutting herself on thorn-bushes in the darkness. She kept on running, not knowing where she was going, until she collapsed to the ground, sobbing with fear and exhaustion.

Yen slept fitfully where she had fallen. But in the cold morning light, she returned to the refuge. It astonished her to see how far she had managed to run in the darkness. The shepherd had already lit a fire. When Yen approached, he did not look at her, but handed her a beaker of hot tea, thickly flavoured with sheep butter. She drank it, and thanked him without rancour. Then the shepherd collected his belongings, and announced: 'We'll go now.'

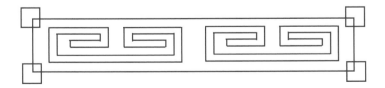

The welcome Yen received at the lamasery was warm and sincere. A lama led her to the nun's hall where she could rest, and spend a few days in quiet contemplation, before entering into the full life of the lamasery.

Yen had been at the lamasery for five days when, unexpectedly, she was told that the High Lama wished to see her. He regarded her kindly, and after a few general remarks, asked if she had any doubts about entering the lamasery.

'None,' replied Yen.

'But you came here under an obligation, not entirely of your own free will. You see, Yen, I know the true reason why you are here. So I will tell you now that the magistrate has released you from your bond – but only on condition that someone else takes your place.'

Seeing her elation, the High Lama held up a cautionary hand. 'But the news may not be so welcome to you. It is Chu-hsin who has chosen to stay here.'

Yen covered her face, trembling. In the short time that the High Lama had been speaking, her emotions had run from serenity to joy, only to plunge into despair. The Lama read her unspoken thoughts. 'If you return to the Great Hall, you will see Chu-hsin for the last time. You may bid him farewell before you leave.'

Never had a few steps taken so long to tread. At last, Yen reached the Great Hall, where a solitary figure, already clad in the russet brown robe of a novice monk, knelt in supplication before the Orpiment Buddha. Choking back her tears, she called Chu-hsin. The novice turned to her. But it was not Chu-hsin – it was the shepherd, his face strangely calm. Yen suddenly understood.

'Hurry down to the river,' the shepherd told her. 'Chu-hsin is waiting for you. I have taken his place.' Then he smiled, adding as a word of explanation: 'A good Dog must always care for his Sheep.'

The Sheep personality

In the Chinese zodiac, the Sheep symbolizes those qualities of human nature that are traditionally regarded as feminine, such as gentleness, consideration for others, and easily expressed emotions. Whether the Sheep personality is male or female, this is a person who has great sympathy for others. The difficulty is that, should the Sheep ever become involved in an unsuitable relationship, the Sheep's over-sensitivity will make it difficult to end the partnership satisfactorily. Equally, of course, once the Sheep has found a true partner, there can be no doubting the depth of sincere affection and love that will hold the couple together.

Both at home and in their working lives, Sheep personalities are apt to be methodical and orderly, always liking everything to be in its place. Organization and regularity are highly important to them. Indeed, there is a danger that they may become slaves to a system. They take great pride in personal appearance, even to the extent of being what some would regard as unnecessarily fussy. In Sheep homes, there are sure to be rooms set aside as show-pieces, and seldom used. But for Sheep-types, these quiet corners are essential havens of tranquillity to which they can escape from a world of turmoil.

Many Sheep personalities have artistic interests. For some, this may be limited to passive involvement, such as listening to music or visiting galleries and museums. Others, however, may pursue their interests actively by playing an instrument, writing or painting. They are more likely to do this for their own amusement, rather than professionally. Nevertheless, those Sheep who feel drawn to the arts as a career should follow their instincts, as most have an undoubted talent for creative work.

Sheep-types like to be thought conventional, but their style often reveals a strong personal identity which is not easily definable. They also tend to reflect current trends, without actually following them. Sheep personalities enjoy company; and whereas some people prefer to get lost in a crowd, the Sheep-type usually manages to achieve the opposite result by using the crowd to advantage.

In many ways, Sheep tend to show more individuality of character than the word 'sheep' would suggest. However, the Chinese word for 'sheep' also means goat, and this is perhaps a clearer indication of the Sheep's independent nature and spirit of adventure.

WHO IS THE PERFECT PARTNER FOR THE SHEEP?

Sometimes, the best companion for someone is a person whose personality is the exact opposite. In such a case, both partners are able to share a wider range of qualities and abilities. Often, too, those whose interests are poles apart attract each other like magnets. This is what is likely to happen when the Sheep character is female, for she is most likely to be physically attracted to a partner whose personality is strongly masculine. But physical attraction is no guarantee of compatibility. Unless there is sound foundation to make the partnership secure, instant passion may soon cool down. Thus the Sheep, dazzled by the glitter and success of the flamboyant Dragon, may be persuaded to do things that are out of character – and come to regret it later.

A relationship with a Dog personality, normally one of the most loyal and faithful of companions, may stagnate unless there are shared interests. The Horse-Sheep relationship, however, bodes well, especially when the Sheep is the female partner. Indeed, there is likely to be a very strong bond between these two companion signs; and once they have settled on each other, they will find it hard to disentangle themselves.

Usually, however, the Sheep prefers to lead a happy and comfortable existence with someone who is more predictable. For, while some people like life to be full of surprises, the Sheep finds it reassuring to know that there will be somebody at hand who can be relied on in times of trouble. Companions who can provide this sort of steadying influence are, above all, the Hare and the Pig. Either of these partners will ensure a stable relationship for the Sheep in their own characteristic ways.

How each of the twelve personality types relates to the Sheep

With THE RAT

A traditional Chinese proverb warns against a Sheep and Rat partnership. Indeed, their characters are frequently so completely different that friends may wonder what it is that they see in each other. If the attraction was instant and physical, it may have been because the Sheep was in a strange or unusual situation, perhaps feeling in need of support. Sometimes, however, a shared interest may draw these two together; but if this is the case, the more personal aspect of the relationship will take time to develop. Theirs is an extraordinary kind of happiness.

With THE OX

The Sheep may regret getting involved in this one-sided relationship. The Ox is by far the stronger partner; and unless the Sheep is perfectly happy to play a subservient role, there could be difficulty in maintaining domestic harmony. It is better when the Sheep is the male partner; but even so, patience with the Ox may wear thin after a while, and resentment at the Ox partner's high-handed manner may erupt over some trifling incident. For this relationship to succeed, the Sheep partner must learn to be more assertive and unafraid of expressing opinions.

With THE TIGER

Bringing excitement into an otherwise routine life, the Tiger exerts a strong attraction for some Sheep personalities. Although this couple may share few interests, the relationship will survive if both accept their individual roles, and perhaps even lead independent lives to a great extent. A long-term commitment is more likely to succeed when the Tiger is the male, perhaps with a career that takes him away from home from time to time, for it is when these two are apart that they most appreciate their need for one another. The Tiger partner will tend to be the leader in this relationship.

With THE HARE

This is one of the best alliances for the Sheep personality; and although it may not be the most exciting of relationships, it is certainly one of the happiest. The partnership is loving, and full of romance, kindness and concern. Both partners are only modestly ambitious; and though they may dream of riches, they will agree that a stable and secure home life is much more important. Their fondness for each other is only matched by their consideration for their children. Hare and Sheep's romantic life may also sometimes be enhanced by a secret language of personal messages, meaningless to outsiders but of great significance to them.

With THE DRAGON

The problem here is that the Dragon is often seen as someone who has achieved everything that the Sheep wanted, if only the Sheep had been blessed with sufficient resources, time or nerve. The Sheep, therefore, looks up to the Dragon as a symbol of success. Indeed, the starry-eyed Sheep may dote on the Dragon, even when it becomes obvious that the Dragon partner is just an ordinary person. However, eventually, the Dragon's special magic is seen to be just an illusion. There is passion in this relationship, but the romance is entirely on the Sheep's side.

With THE SNAKE

This may not be the Sheep's most compatible partner, but there is enough trust and understanding on both sides for the two to live together in harmony. Both are romantic creatures at heart, for whom mental stimulus is as important as physical attraction. Indeed, they probably got to know each other through shared interests. The Sheep will find the Snake considerate and appreciative of the Sheep's caring nature. The physical side of love is not forgotten, although both may feel, at times, that there are heights yet to be scaled.

With THE HORSE

If the Sheep is the female partner, this relationship will be firm, with a strong – essentially physical – bond, which both find stimulating and fulfilling. Yet although there is a tremendous animal attraction between these two passionate partners when they meet, they may be economical with the time they spend together. The male Horse partner may be engaged in business or in the armed services, which takes him away from home for long periods. And, likewise, should the Sheep be the male partner, the exciting companionship of the female Horse may not always be present. For even when there is no unavoidable situation holding these two apart, their life-styles and personal interests may be so different that they lead virtually separate lives. Whatever the circumstances, the Horse-type is likely to be the dominant partner in this relationship.

With ANOTHER SHEEP

A happy and prosperous existence is in store for two Sheep personalities, who are likely to become completely wrapped up in each other. Their life-style may be predictable, but rather than this being a weak point in their relationship, it is a source of strength. Their outlook on life is similar, and they will share many interests outside the home. Indeed, they probably met through being members of the same society or leisure group. Their love for each other will be deep and fulfilling, for each understands the other's needs perfectly.

With THE MONKEY

This is one of those difficult personality clashes when two types, with such differing views, nevertheless have enough in common to draw them together. The Monkey has much to offer the Sheep by way of material help and mental support, but demands a lot in return. As a result, the Sheep is often left wondering whether life would be better without the Monkey partner, even though separation would be painful. In the end, the Sheep may think that such problems are preferable to loneliness. Their love involves passion rather than romance. Indeed, it is a strongly physical relationship, transcending rational explanation.

With THE ROOSTER

This may not be the most ideal of partnerships, but as long as it lasts, it will be a fulfilling experience for both zodiac types; and though there may be some problems along the way, the Sheep will certainly be wiser as a result. The Rooster and Sheep may have been thrown together by circumstances, rather than choice, and it may take time for any physical chemistry to take effect. A long courtship may not be a bad idea, however: it will give this couple ample time to find out if they are really suited. Despite the Rooster being a flamboyant and forceful character, it is probably the Sheep that leads the way in this partnership. Providing the Sheep makes allowances for the Rooster's basic personality profile and the Rooster comes to understand the value of compromise, they should be happy together.

With THE DOG

Could this be the Sheep's worst choice for a life companion? The Dog personality may be doing its utmost to look after the Sheep's best interests; but as a rule, the Sheep personality is unlikely to be grateful. A conflict of interests, with both parties believing they know what is best for the other, can hardly provide much by way of a suitable foundation for a harmonious partnership. Their love life could thus be difficult, fraught with misunderstandings. Romance could easily go astray, for the physical needs of one never seem coincide with those of the partner. If the relationship is to succeed, the Dog will need to come to understand that the Sheep resents being dominated to any degree. Then it stands a good chance of lasting.

With THE PIG

The Sheep personality who wants a happy, stable domestic life, a caring environment for raising a family, and a comfortable home, could find no better partner than the Pig. With a well-deserved reputation for looking after others, the Pig is an ideal homemaker who will ensure that the Sheep is freed from worries and anxieties. This is a couple who have found the happy medium between a life of hard work and a life of comfort. Their love is deep and strong.

CHAPTER NINE
THE MONKEY

Running water does not get stagnant

The beggar girl emptied her pockets, and put a clutch of copper coins on the stone bench. 'How much did you get?' she asked her companion, without any sign of optimism.

Ku-mien threw down a few coins of his own.

'Is that all? What good is that? cried the girl in disbelief.

'That's it. I've been everywhere, Tian. The market, the temple, the harbour. No one seems to have any money these days.'

'The city is full of people with money!' snapped Tian. 'It's just that you don't look in the right places. Rich people won't be in the market buying cabbages, or hanging around the harbour looking for work. They'll be in the jade market, in Silk Street, or in the Fragrant Stream Gardens.'

'And you expect me to get anywhere near those places in these rags?' Ku-mien retorted.

'What about me? cried Tian. 'I suppose you think I look like a mandarin's wife in these tattered things.'

'You look better than I do. That's probably why no one gives you money either - you look too good!'

Tia softened. 'Do I really?' she asked, kissing him affectionately.
'It's when you don't mean to be kind to me
that you're nicest to me.

'That's what I like about you. Now, don't worry about the money for the moment. Let's go to the inn. You can drink some wine; and while you're doing that, I shall think of a plan.'

Ku-mien groaned inwardly, for Tian's plans usually involved work of some kind or other. Still, he allowed himself to be taken to the inn, certain that the cash they had collected would pay for ample wine. But Ku-mien would have been even less cheerful if he had known that going to the inn was actually part of Tian's latest strategy.

Tian herself did not take more than one cup – the better, she always said, to keep a clear head. This arrangement was perfectly satisfactory for Ku-mien, since it left more wine for himself; and just as Tian had planned, it was not long before he had reached a state of benign amnesia.

Tian waited until she judged Ku-mien to be sufficiently insensible, and then led him away from the inn to a neighbourhood where several rich merchants lived. She propped Ku-mien against the wall, quickly stripped all the clothes from his body, and hid them. Then she began to scream for help.

Within moments, a number of servants had hurried from the house to see the cause of the disturbance. The householder followed.
Tian ran up to him, sobbing hysterically.
'Oh, the poor man!' she wailed. 'Please help him!' He saw some villains who were climbing your wall to rob your house. But when he tried to stop them, they attacked him instead, and took everything he had... even the clothes he stood up in.
'Heavens! Who is he?' cried the merchant.
'I really have no idea, Sir,' Tian replied. 'But let someone put some clothes on him, at least!'

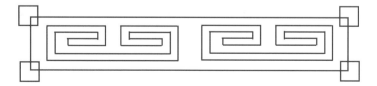

Ku-mien rubbed his head painfully and sat up, mystified. For reasons he could not understand, he was now wearing new clothes.
'What's all this?' he asked Tian, indignantly. 'Where did the money for such garb come from? Are you mad, woman? I can't go out begging dressed like this. People will be asking *me* for money! The best thing I can do is take this lot and try to sell it in the market.'

Tian was hurt, but she was not the sort of girl to let herself be upset by her lover's selfishness. She decided instead to go the Fragrant Stream Gardens herself. Though she would not be allowed in the more exclusive parts of the gardens, there were several areas open to all.

She had not gone far, when a voice called out to her: 'Tell your fortune, Miss?'
She turned, and was surprised to see that the fortune-teller was quite a young man. She gave a regretful shrug. 'No money, I'm afraid.'
He smiled. 'That doesn't matter. Just sit down for a while. You might attract a few paying customers.'
Amused, Tian joined the young man. He examined her face and palm, and asked then for details of her date of birth.

'I know that I was born in the year of the Monkey,' she said.
'Ah! That explains it,' said the fortune-teller. 'You have been having some problems recently with your present lover. Is he, astrologically speaking of course, a Pig?'
'Why, yes!' exclaimed Tian. 'But aren't a Pig and Monkey suited?'
'No,' replied the fortune-teller. 'You need the protection of someone such as me, a Dog.'

'If you're trying to drop a hint, I should tell you that I'm already spoken for.' She tactfully changed the subject, observing: 'I think you would get more clients if you had a more attractive sign.

Before he had time to take offence, she took his brush and paper, and swiftly painted a most professional-looking trade card.

'That's my payment for your services. Now I must go and find my Pig.' She rose and left; but when she looked over her shoulder a few minutes later, she was gratified to see her new friend surrounded by a group of potential customers.

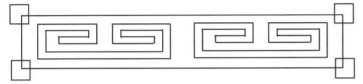

The fine weather had brought many to the gardens, and Tian had no difficulty in collecting enough to buy herself a reasonable meal at the lakeside tea-house. She was about to go in when she saw Ku-mien, slouched over a table, in close company with a young woman whose reputation was widely known. Shocked, Tian hurried away, blind and deaf to everything around her.

Suddenly Tian was pulled up short by two rough men. She struggled, but suddenly recognized one of the men.

He stared at her closely, and shouted: 'I've seen this girl before. She was with that man who swindled old Wu out of a set of clothes last night.'

Tian protested innocence, but the man gloated. He gave his companion a knowing look; and twisting Tian's arm behind her back, held on to her firmly. 'Now you can either come back quietly with us to Mr Wu's house, and explain to him what you were up to, or you can carry on screaming while we take you to the magistrate. Which is it to be?'

Reluctantly, Tian let herself be hauled away under arrest. It was degrading enough to be a spectacle for the strollers, but most shameful of all was being dragged in disgrace past the young fortune-teller who had befriended her earlier. He chanced to glance up and saw her being forcibly led away. His face was blank and uncomprehending.

The men led Tian from the gardens to a shabby house close by. 'This isn't the house,' she declared. But the men pushed her into a dank, windowless room, and closed the doors behind them. The man she had recognized leered at her suggestively.

'I know what sort of woman you are,' he smirked. 'So why don't you do yourself a favour, and be nice to me and my friend here. Then we can forget all about your little tricks at Wu's house. No need to make your mind up yet. But don't take too long about it.'

The two men laughed coarsely and left her, bolting the door behind them.

As soon as she heard them leave the house, Tian went to the door, but could not open it from the inside. It seemed that for once in her life, she was without a plan.

Soon, fortified by wine, the men returned. The older man threw back the bolts, and stared into the room, then exclaimed: 'She's hiding behind the table. Come on out, you fool!'

Suddenly, he staggered and fell to the ground as a violent kick struck him in the face. His companion leapt to one side, but it was too late to avoid the blow to the back of his neck. Before they had time to recover, Tian and the fortune-teller had run out, slamming and bolting the door behind them.

They fled from the house, and did not stop running until they had reached a quiet street.

Breathless, they collapsed to the ground and burst out laughing. 'If you hadn't followed me, I don't know what would have happened,' said Tian.

'I can guess,' replied her new friend. 'He got quite a shock when he found a man behind the table. But not as much as when you dropped from the ceiling,' continued the young man, admiringly. 'Where on earth did you learn that trick?'

'Would you believe me if I said I used to be an acrobat?'

'After that, I'd believe anything.'

Then he leant over and kissed her; and for a long time, they said nothing more at all.

The Monkey personality

The Monkey symbolizes agility – not only physical suppleness or manual dexterity, but quickness of mind, ready wit, and an ability to twist difficult situations to advantage. Monkey personalities may reveal this through an interest in technical matters, and instinctive skills with gadgets and tools. So it is that some Monkey-types combine hands and brain to make first-rate jewellers or surgeons; while others, with the gifts of rhetoric and logic, may enter the legal profession to make excellent lawyers.

The Monkey King is one of the favourite characters from Chinese fiction, being a mischievous creature who seems out of control, until he reforms and helps bring the Buddhist scriptures to China. Mischief and a scorn for authority are, indeed, the negative sides of the Monkey's qualities – although the Monkey would probably regard these as virtues. After all, many of the Monkey's cunning schemes are merely quick and effective ways to settle scores without having to resort either to violence or the courts.

But perhaps the gravest danger facing the Monkey personality is the temptation to deceive; for, with such an agile mind, the Monkey soon becomes aware just how gullible most people are.

Indeed, while positive Monkey-types may dedicate their skills to the welfare or benefit of others, some Monkeys may find it all too easy to make fools of those around them. Yet it would be wrong to think that they were deliberately malicious; rather, they tend to feel that if opportunities exist, they should be taken.

A common frustration for Monkey personalities is that, having such an air of nonchalance and light-heartedness, when they do have something of importance to offer, they are sometimes not taken seriously. For the career-minded Monkey, whose early ambitions are frequently thereby thwarted, this can cause deep and long-lasting resentment. At home, too, relationships sometimes take a turn for the worse, simply because the Monkey is not someone who takes kindly to any advice that is offered.

But the Monkey soon learns the hard way, and lessons are not forgotten. As the Monkey becomes older and wiser, it is likely to gain in prestige and win the respect it deserves. In personal relationships, too, the Monkey may become more knowledgeable than most about human nature, eventually acquiring a self-confidence that is to be admired.

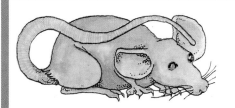
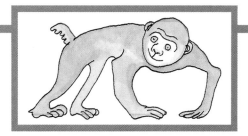

WHO IS THE PERFECT PARTNER FOR THE MONKEY?

It is hard for anyone not to enjoy the company of the mischievous and light-hearted Monkey. But for those who are not entirely in tune with the Monkey's high spirits, its antics may prove wearing after a while. Those most suited to be the Monkey's partner will be keen to share in its adventurous activities, and benefit from the mental or emotional stimulation that it readily provides. The two most obvious candidates are the night-loving Rat personality, and the magnetic Dragon-type. And what an energetic and forceful couple the Monkey and Dragon might make!

But whose company would most benefit the Monkey when it comes to a stable and loving relationship? It is one thing to live the high life with a like-minded companion, but quite another to face the serious issues of living and raising a family. The Monkey really needs someone who can share in its sense of fun and spirit of adventure, but who at the same time is able to provide steady support. But a partner who is too staid and hidebound could make the Monkey restless, thereby wasting all good intentions and possibly risking inevitable separation. That is why the astrologers of old had nothing positive to say in favour of a choice such as the Ox – far too cautious for the intrepid Monkey – or for the stern and disapproving figure of the Tiger. Nor is the Pig usually a suitable partner. As a Chinese proverb puts it: 'Monkey and Pig always end in tears'.

A far more suitable personality can be found in the Dog-type, who as a rule is defensive and supportive, without being too conventional. Another partner who will complement the Monkey to good effect is the hard-working and diligent Horse-type.

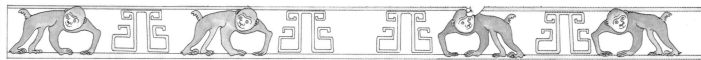

How each of the twelve personality types relates to the Monkey

With THE RAT
This should be a very successful partnership for the Monkey personality, the more so if the Monkey is the male partner. But even when the Monkey partner is the female, the special talents and ingenuity of her Rat companion will prove advantageous. Both in business and at home, this couple will be mutually supportive, and their love for each other will be extremely fulfilling. Because of similar past experiences, both types find that they are able to understand each other's problems particularly well.

With THE OX
This may not be the ideal relationship for the Monkey – since the Monkey and Ox might not share as many interests as some couples – but they are able to follow their pursuits without jealousy or resentment. The Monkey will find the Ox partner supportive in practical matters and, if a little too predictable, a source of strength in times of trouble. The Monkey personality can, in return, provide stimulation and excitement. Their initial physical attraction is likely to mature into deeper understanding.

With THE TIGER
The Monkey personality may admire the Tiger from afar, but should think twice about getting too close. An old Chinese proverb declares: 'He who rides a Tiger finds it hard to dismount'. The Tiger is too authoritarian, or too dismissive, for the Monkey to develop a close and warm relationship. But this may improve once there is an addition to the family; and harmony and stability are assured if their child is born in the year of the Rat, Dragon, Horse or Dog. They will be too concerned about the welfare of the newcomer to bother about differences that used to exist between them. The physical side of their love ought to be stimulating, though the Tiger may not always agree as to what constitutes a fulfilling relationship.

With THE HARE
Here is a couple who are ever youthful. Friends may think they are completely mismatched, but they will grow together with time. Each has much to learn about the other; as a result, life together is continually stimulating. The Hare is supportive and realistic, which is often vital where the Monkey is concerned. One of the problems that may arise in this relationship is that the Monkey may tend to make all the decisions, without consulting the Hare partner. Naturally, this can lead to problems, and even the Hare – normally the most mild-mannered of companions – cannot help feeling resentful after a while. As quick-thinking as the Monkey is, patience and consideration will go a long way towards keeping this relationship as warm and loving as it ought to be.

With THE DRAGON
What an exciting partnership this is! Whatever the Monkey wants to do in life, there could be no better help-mate than the charismatic and adventurous Dragon. There should be plenty of time, too, for romance, passion and frequent travel. All this seems to rule out a stable family life, since domesticity is not for this daredevil couple. The physical side of their love is sure to be wildly passionate – although there is a danger that they could drain each other emotionally.

With THE SNAKE
The Snake exudes a dangerous charm and fascination for the Monkey. And given the Monkey's spirit of adventure and general recklessness, together they could be tempted into situations that could be disastrous. Despite its outward cleverness, the Monkey is naive in many ways, and could easily be deceived and hurt by the Snake. But the Monkey quickly learns through experience, and if these two can survive some initial difficulties, it will not be long before they build a lasting partnership on equal terms.

With THE HORSE

This is one of the Monkey's happier relationships. The Horse partner will be devoted and faithful – so much so that if circumstances force this couple apart for any length of time, it causes a great deal of distress for both of them. The Horse provides security, comfort and financial stability for the Monkey partner who offers both stimulation and encouragement in return. There is no doubting the love that these two have for each other, founded as it is in romantic idealism, physical attraction, the need for companionship and loyalty. But the benefits are not confined to home and family; for the Monkey and the Horse bring each other a confidence which is happily reflected by success in their respective careers.

With THE SHEEP

If the Sheep manages to stay a long-time partner of the Monkey, it is because both accept their various differences and in due course come to terms with them. Life-styles, opinions and even personal behaviour are so contrasting that, early in the relationship, both partners must learn to make allowances for each other's preferences. These two personality types need plenty of space – mentally and physically – for them to develop their own individuality. If they are following different careers in the outside world, problems between them are unlikely to arise. However, at home, where they are inevitably in close contact, they both need to have moments of privacy and allowance should be made for this.

With ANOTHER MONKEY

A partnership of like minds, two Monkeys make exhilarating company for each other. In careers and leisure activities, they follow similar lines; they may even have met through being members of the same organization. Still, they are both probably highly individualistic, and while agreeing over most things in broad principle, it is a different matter when it comes down to details. In love, their relationship is likely to be more physical than emotional, for both tend to put personal needs before consideration for the partner. Both therefore need to become less self-centred.

With THE ROOSTER

Whether this is a business partnership or a romance, Rooster and Monkey personalities will almost certainly find that they are a close match. Both may work towards the same goal, and have highly individualistic skills and abilities which complement each other well. The Monkey and Rooster are drawn together magnetically, and their physical love is usually exceptionally satisfying. Almost certainly, their children will benefit, too, from having such well-matched parents who will, nevertheless, succeed in maintaining a degree of independence so that neither partner is smothered.

With THE DOG

This relationship may turn out to be an unexpectedly successful one. Although the Dog and Monkey appear on the surface to have entirely different life-styles, there is something in their personalities that draws them together. This may be a need for companionship more than physical attraction – probably the reason why this partnership generally has such a solid foundation. Should this couple ever split up, they are likely to remain on friendly terms; indeed, they may even get together again and find their partnership becomes all the stronger due to a period apart. The family is unlikely to suffer as a result of such a temporary parting either. The emotional side of their love life is far more important than the physical, and more enduring.

With THE PIG

Traditionally, this is one of the partnerships that ought to be avoided. Indeed, there are said to be too many conflicts of opinion, especially with regard to priorities. Unless both the Monkey and the Pig understand the extent and limitations of their responsibilities, the partnership could break down. Often, the Monkey's ambitions are set much higher than the Pig can accept. And while the Pig may want to establish a firm base at home, the Monkey could find this too restraining. If the relationship is not to end in tears, they need to compromise considerably – the Pig, for example, learning to tolerate the Monkey's many moods.

CHAPTER TEN

THE ROOSTER

Ripples in an old well

The autumn sun dipped and touched the horizon. Long, crimson ribbons stretched across the western sky, turning the River Lo to the colour of ruby wine. In the east, the moon was bright and golden. All Heaven was a blaze of colour.

Ssu-pin went to her window, breathing in the perfume of late orchids. Tomorrow evening would be the night of the Autumn Moon Festival, when all over China friends gather together in their gardens to watch for the full moon. She, too, had invited some old friends; and to make the evening more spectacular, she was having a moon-viewing terrace constructed on the eastern slope of her garden. There, her guests could sit, eat delicious moon cakes, drink wine, and compete in the composition of witty poems – all by the light of red candles, lanterns, and the harvest moon at its most brilliant.

Ssu-pin felt that she ought to prepare some quotations to be the subjects of poems for tomorrow's guests. Her writing-set was already laid out on the rosewood table, but she had no inclination to do anything. She sighed. Autumn's beauty was magnificent, but she knew that its splendours marked the onset of winter's bitterness. How long, she wondered, would it be before she reached the autumn of her own years?

As Ssu-pin looked towards the new terrace, she was surprised to see a man still working there, even though the sun had almost set.

'You may finish for today,' she called out to him.

He looked up towards her, and then glanced back again at his work, seemingly reluctant to leave it. She called again.

'Can you not complete it tomorrow? You must be wanting to return home.'

'No,' he replied in a resigned tone. 'There's no urgency. I had hoped to finish the balustrade tonight; there isn't much more to be done. But the light is fading. I'll come back early in the morning if you prefer.'

Ssu-pin looked at him enquiringly. 'You aren't the man I engaged to work.'

'No, that was Old Chieh, my father. I'm Young Chieh. As the terrace has to be finished before your guests arrive, I came to help him.'

'And he has left you to finish his work,' laughed Ssu-pin.

'He has a wife to go home to. I don't.'

Ssu-pin was surprised. Somehow, he gave her the impression of being a married man. But there was something in his tone which prevented her enquiring further. She turned to more practical matters.

'You must be hungry, Chieh. Have you eaten today?' She glanced into the dining-room. 'Perhaps you would give me your opinion on my moon cakes?'

He looked down at his grimy tunic. Ssu-pin smiled, understanding. 'Look, why don't you wash yourself by the well,' she told him. 'Then come to the kitchen.'

Ssu-pin heard Chieh's footsteps as he returned from the well. He stood in the doorway, so transformed that she was momentarily startled. Although his tunic was rough and torn, he had an imposing bearing; his black hair shone, and now that the grime had gone from his face, Ssu-pin could see that he still kept the handsome features of his youth.

'You could eat here, but I wanted to discuss the work that still has to be done. If you were to eat on the moon terrace,' she smiled, 'it would be a rehearsal for tomorrow. That would be the best way to see if anything has been overlooked.'

He appeared pleased. 'Why yes, we must make sure that everything is perfect.'

He carried a table and chairs to the terrace, and set down the tray. He gave Ssu-pin a quizzical look.

'What do people actually do on moon terraces?' he asked her. She motioned him to sit down.

'Well, they first eat something; then, perhaps, they take some wine.' She poured samshu into two cups. 'And then, they look at the moon.'

While they drank, Ssu-pin told him of the legend that had inspired the traditional Moon-watching ceremony.

'The story is that once there was a beautiful woman, Chang O, whose husband was a brave and famous archer. The Goddess of the Western Sky gave him a pill that would make him immortal. But Chang O found it, and ate it out of curiosity. Immediately, she was transported through the air, to the moon, where she lives to this day. Now, every year, when the moon is brightest and fullest, those who are lucky in love will see her.'

Chieh looked at her, charmed by the simple story. 'I've never seen her, though,' Ssu-pin added, wistfully. 'But I still watch.' At this point, she decided to ask the question that had been troubling her: 'And you, Chieh. You said you had no wife to go home to. I can't believe you never married.'

'I was married,' he replied without emotion. 'But my wife died a few years ago.'

'I'm sorry,' Ssu-pin replied, with genuine sympathy. 'Do you have any children?'

'A boy, four years old, and a girl of ten. My parents look after them when I am away. But what about you? Don't you have a husband?'

'It's a long story,' she replied. 'And not as pretty as the one about Chang O.'

Ssu-pin took a taper, and lit a lantern. In its yellow flame, the shadows of chrysanthemums danced and flickered on the screen beside her. 'Will you ever marry?' he asked her.

'No ripples in an old well,' she replied.

'What does that mean?' he asked her.

'It means I am no longer young; no longer liable to be thrown into turmoil by some passing infatuation.'

Chieh sipped at the samshu. 'Some people find love early in life. Others must wait longer.'

'They say that true love is decided according to the laws of Heaven,' said Ssu-pin. 'If you marry someone whose birth sign is in harmony with your own – mine is the Rooster – then you will find peace and happiness. And to think that the moon up there could be shining on the one person I might share my life with.'

'Perhaps,' remarked her companion, 'he is looking at the moon even now, thinking the same thing.'

'And you?' asked Ssu-pin. 'What is your birth sign?'

'I was born in the year of the Ox.'

'That explains why you're so strong.'

The two people sat strangely thoughtful, watching the moon.

'Those flecks and shadows,' said Chieh. 'It is curious, but when you look at them in a certain way, they do seem to take on the features of a face. Could that be Chang O?'

'We are a night early, remember,' said Ssu-pin. 'This is only a rehearsal.' But it was certainly remarkable how clear the moon's face was that evening. It was odd, too, that for as long as she could remember, she had never actually sat, and gazed so contentedly.

'And when your guests have watched the moon, will they then write poems about it?' Chieh asked.

'It's an old custom,' she explained. 'Sometimes the inspiration comes naturally; sometimes it has to be jolted. Tomorrow, I will give the guests the opening lines for them to complete. It's just a nice way to pass the time. I'll show you. Give me an idea for a poem.'

'What about the phrase you used earlier: Ripples in an old well?'

Ssu-pin considered his suggestion for a moment.

'The well is old, the water still.
I see Chang O's face
Reflected in the water.'

Chieh suddenly took her hand, and replied.

'The well is old, the water still.
A bucket drops in the water.
Even Chang O can see the ripples.'

Ssu-pin said nothing; then, to Chieh's distress, she burst into tears. Without thinking, he caught hold of her hand to comfort her. She fell on to his shoulder, weeping openly, yet all the while not knowing why.

Chieh stroked her hair affectionately, turned her face towards his and kissed away her salt tears. She held him closely. It may have been the illusion of love that she felt within her, but she knew the memory of that moment would never fade. Softly, she drifted into sleep.

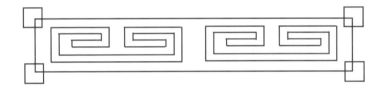

When Ssu-pin eventually woke, Chieh was gently cradling her head in his arms, fearful of disturbing her rest.

'Will you marry me?' were his first words as she opened her eyes.

Ssu-pin did not respond at once but shook her head slowly. 'Wait at least until the night has passed. In the morning, by the light of day, you will know your true feelings.'

From a distant farmhouse, a rooster crowed to greet the dawn.

'It is already morning,' he replied. 'My true feelings are no different now than from the first moment I saw you standing by your window. Ssu-pin, will you marry me?'

'Yes, I will,' she replied.

The Rooster personality

The Rooster personality is shrewd yet rather extravagant at times, considerate but abrasive, stylish but disdainful of affectation. Typically, too, the Rooster quickly polarizes people into opposing factions. Others will always have a ready opinion of a Rooster personality, whether good or bad, and it is generally only other Roosters who find it difficult to make a subjective judgement of each other.

Rooster personalities are often gifted with sound business acumen, an eye for current trends, and a determination to succeed in whatever they put their minds to. But a failing frequently lies in their occasional need to make dramatic and extravagant gestures, which may cause financial problems if badly timed.

Roosters are gifted with a real sense of style. They pay great attention to their personal appearance, being extremely particular in their choice of clothes; indeed, they are sometimes so finnicky about their grooming that it may be misconstrued as vanity. Roosters are also careful about their health and physical well being – even their poise. Always anxious to make a good impression, the Rooster will strive to be an inspiring conversationalist, too.

To this end, Rooster personalities are often avid readers of journals and magazines, which help them to keep in touch with world events.

Most of the 'feminine' or yin zodiac signs of Chinese astrology (Ox, Hare, Snake, Sheep, Rooster and Pig) tend to have a 'soft' side to their characters, but Rooster men prove an exception. Indeed, their masculine, competitive traits are actually sharpened. They may even give the impression of being constantly burdened by some long-standing resentment. The male Rooster-type also tends to find it more difficult t o establish firm and lasting friendships than the females of this animal sign.

All Rooster personalities distinguish themselves by their liveliness and enthusiasm; and once they have set themselves on a particular course of action, it would be foolhardy to try and deter them from it. With their boundless energy, they are unlikely to have much patience for those who do not share their high standards of perfection. They will quickly reject anything that they find unacceptable, but will be highly defensive of those who are less able or disadvantaged; and, characteristically, will never refuse help to those who are genuinely in need.

WHO IS THE PERFECT PARTNER FOR THE ROOSTER?

The Rooster is one of the few exceptions to the general rule that two people born under the same sign are compatible: for not only do two Rooster personalities create difficulties for each other, they will tend to create problems for everyone around them. But finding the right partner for the Rooster is not easy. While they certainly enjoy the company of others and are highly social animals, lasting relationships can be elusive. The Rooster is not easily pleased, and few potential partners are able to fulfil their very exacting demands. Moreover, those who are able to offer the excitement and stimulus in which the Rooster delights are unlikely to provide the steadying influence which the Rooster needs; while those who are able to be supportive are likely to be rejected by the Rooster as essentially unadventurous.

The trouble for the Rooster is that when someone does come along who is absolutely right, this ideal partner is, unfortunately, often already attached to someone else. The Rooster's best chances of a permanent relationship are to find the right person early on in life, or to hope that opportunity calls a second time.

In the Chinese horoscope chart, the Rooster's two most suitable partners are the Ox and the Snake. Intellectually, the Rooster will find the Snake the more interesting companion; but on a physical level, the somewhat down-to-earth Ox may have surprising talents which certainly compensate for someone who otherwise appears staid and matter-of-fact. Both these types will be able to offer the security that such a volatile personality requires. If the Rooster is female, then the Ox partner would be the better choice; for the male Rooster, the Snake.

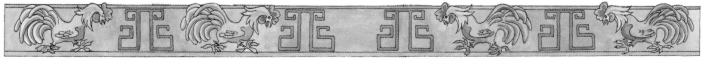

How each of the twelve personality types relates to the Rooster

With THE RAT

The Rat and the Rooster may admire each other's qualities, but they have wills of their own. Though they share many qualities, and may be able to co-operate, there are many issues on which they differ. They both need excitement in their lives – but, unfortunately, they are unlikely to be excited by the same things. The Rooster may also consider the Rat too introspective and over-cautious. This will be a partnership of two people who place great value on independence, and there is a danger that a relationship that is too restricting could ultimately crack unless care is taken.

With THE OX

For the female Rooster, this is one of the best partners she could find – brooding, mysterious, and in many ways the Mr Right of romantic fiction. For the male Rooster, too, an Ox partner embodies all the sensual charms of his fantasies. On the surface, the choice may seem an unlikely one for the brash and lively Rooster. What could such a stubborn traditionalist have that could attract the ebullient Rooster? The answer lies much deeper, for there is hidden passion lurking under that innocuous exterior. The Ox, it is said, is the only animal that can overpower all the others; and this sign is almost certain to conquer the Rooster's heart.

With THE TIGER

There is no doubt that this couple will be the centre of attraction whenever they are seen together. Both are leaders in their own fields; and with a zest for living, they certainly belong with the fast set. But whether this relationship is the ideal one is another matter. There may be sadness, disappointment and anxiety hidden behind those glamorous clothes and flashing smiles. Indeed, they will need to work hard at developing a warmer relationship, and to be frank and open with each other, instead of trying to live the kind of life that they think may be expected of them.

With THE HARE

The Rooster may be quite happy to be the dominant partner in this relationship, but it would be foolish to assume that the Hare feels the same way. While the Hare may be attracted at first by the Rooster's verve and style, it is hard to stay the pace. This partnership has a greater chance of success if the two are separated from time to time, perhaps because of career commitments. Such an arrangement will be greatly to the Hare's advantage, but possibly not acceptable to the Rooster. Nevertheless, physically, these partners are frequently highly compatible.

With THE DRAGON

For a whirlwind romance, excitement and a heady, passionate relationship, the Dragon partner will prove ideal for the Rooster. But if the Rooster is looking for a long-term commitment, marriage, and someone who can take a positive role in sharing the responsibilities of family life, then this relationship may not prove so successful. Both are highly motivated individuals, with independent natures who – though caring about each other – are unlikely to give up those aspects of their lives they feel are most important – whether these are career, family or social commitments.

With THE SNAKE

This could be a wonderful partner for the Rooster. Although the relationship works best of all when the Rooster is the male partner, the female Rooster can still rely on this partnership to be one of the happiest, most enduring and fulfilling that she is likely to find. For the female Rooster, the initial attraction is an intellectual one; while the male Rooster will find his Snake partner sensuously attractive. With time, the couple begin to discover each other's hidden depths, and will become bonded indissolubly. Yet this is not just a marriage of minds, for there is promise of physical fulfilment which should last long after the honeymoon is over.

With THE HORSE

The Rooster's attraction to the Horse could soon fade away unless the Horse is prepared considerably to modify its brash self-assurance. Nearly always the male partner in this relationship, the Horse is likely to be too much of a chauvinist to hold the Rooster's devotion for long, and so must be wary of becoming a bore. The same applies if the Horse is the female partner: the constant repetitions of her views on social issues and other affairs could tire even the most ardent Rooster after a while. This couple really needs to decide that they are a partnership, and not just two individuals who have thrown themselves together to see how long the relationship can last.

With THE SHEEP

Whatever the circumstances were that made companions of this couple, they would probably like to think it was destiny that drew them together. But whether it was sharing a career or the same apartment block – or merely being thrust together during a long and tedious journey – that triggered the relationship, there remains a wide gulf in their respective personalities. The Rooster has such a powerful personality, and the Sheep such an introspective view of life, that there seems to be little for each to offer the other. However, the relationship could prove much more successful if the Sheep is shown trust and allowed to lead the way occasionally.

With THE MONKEY

This couple are such a close match that it is not surprising that they may seem to have found an ideal life's companion. Not only do they have many varied interests in common, each has specific abilities and imaginative ideas which will stimulate a working and romantic relationship. The only problem with this relationship is that both partners may become so wrapped up in each other that they tend to lose touch with the world outside. They need, occasionally, to take, and not resent, advice from friends and others concerned for their welfare. On the whole, however, they should encounter no problems in establishing a long and happy family life.

With ANOTHER ROOSTER

Most couples born under the same astrological sign are able to live happily together, but this is rarely the case with two Roosters. They know themselves far too well, and will only too readily spot their own faults reflected in their partners. Not unexpectedly, it hurts not being able to reprimand or criticize each other without being shown up as a hypocrite. As a result, there is likely to be a lot of tension in the air, which occasionally explodes, especially if these two live in very confined accommodation. They need their own space, and this relationship will work much better if they are able to act independently at times. Mutual respect must be nurtured.

With THE DOG

This couple are likely to come from the same background, have the same friends, and share many similar interests. But like two colours which are almost a match, there is something about the partnership that interferes with prospect of true compatibility. Indeed, when it comes to taking a big decision – perhaps a holiday venue, a place to live or an important change in career – disagreement may prove so strong that the idea is abandoned altogether. It therefore becomes vital for them to agree who is going to make the decisions, and then to abide by this. Not surprisingly, the love-life of a Dog and Rooster is likely to be volatile.

With THE PIG

This partnership has every possibility of becoming highly successful, especially if the Rooster is the breadwinner in the household, and the Pig is allowed to get on with the very important business of building a comfortable home for them both. But just because the Pig shows relatively little interest in the Rooster's career, this does not mean that the Pig is uninterested in the welfare of the Rooster. There is sure to be much love, understanding and warmth in this relationship, as different as these two personalities may seem to be from the point of view of an outsider. Nevertheless, happy and contented children will provide clear evidence that the affection between Pig and Rooster parents is genuine.

CHAPTER ELEVEN

THE DOG

Riding a horse to look for a horse

With trembling fingers, Fei took the letter from the messenger and handed it to her father. Although she could not read the characters, she recognized the clusters of intricate strokes that together formed the name Hua Lung. Her father put down the bowl he was varnishing, looked at the packet with some distaste, and passed it to his wife.

'A letter!' he said, annoyed at having to give a handful of copper coins to the messenger. 'Who would want to write to us?'

A look of alarm crossed Fei's face as her mother smoothed the wrappings with fingers damp from the kitchen. 'Please don't smudge it,' she pleaded. 'Otherwise we won't be able to read it.'

'Can't read it anyway,' was the brusque riposte. 'We'll have to get old Chao, the astrologer, to read it to us. Or why don't you ask that nice student who's always hanging around here? What's his name? Pao Tai?'

'Pao Tai?' asked Fei. 'But the letter might be... for me.' Fei blushed. Pao Tai was the last person she wanted reading her private letters.

'For you!' cried her mother, wonderingly. 'I hardly think so!'

'But that's Hua Lung's name. I know!'

'Is it indeed?' said her father, his eyebrows raised in amusement. 'So you can read now?'

Fei bowed her head in embarrassment, and pointed to the few characters that she recognized. 'Hua Lung always promised he would write when he went away.'

'Well, it's taken him long enough,' answered her mother grudgingly. She had never liked the youth, with his foppish ways and affected manners. Fei, however, doted on him. But her mother considered his charms to be nothing more than a thin veneer. As far as anyone knew, he had gone off to the city to be an actor, and had never been heard of since. Good riddance, she thought.

Fei's father, however, was rather more impressed. This was the first time he had ever known Fei to decipher characters, and if she could make out the words 'Hua' and 'Lung', she could surely learn to read other characters, too. A daughter who could read and write would be a great asset. And as for this Hua Lung, the actor, actors become famous and make lots of money, he mused. Who knows, actors are sometimes invited to court, and if Hua Lung married their Fei...

While musing, he had resumed his varnishing. Suddenly, he snapped out of his day-dream and turned to the more immediate problem.

'Well, daughter! I think we'd better get this letter read. And replied to, if need be. I don't suppose you know what it says?'

To his disappointment, though not surprise, she did not. With a sigh, her father realized he was going to have to send for the astrologer – or the student. Despite Fei's protestations, he decided on the student. It would be cheaper.

Pao Tai was a jovial man, in his mid-twenties, which made him about eight years older than Fei. Although Fei's mother always spoke of him as a student, he was hardly a scholar. Pao Tai's father had high hopes that his son could pass the examinations and become a mandarin. But Pao Tai did not relish being cooped up in a study. He much preferred to be outside, riding under the blazing sun, or swimming in the cool water of the Lo River.

Somewhat reluctantly, Fei followed her father's bidding, and walked across the fields to the village where Pao Tai lodged. She scorned her mother's description of him as a student; how could he possibly be compared with Hua Lung? He may have been able to read, but he was no more than a farmhand – without a trace of elegance, grace or breeding.

Hua Lung, by contrast, was quite different. He could recite from the classics and turn words into poetry just by speaking. Fei reached up and jangled the chime.

Pao Tai was delighted to see Fei. Within the past twelve months, she had blossomed from being an ungainly, dumpy girl into a truly beautiful young woman. What a pity, he thought, that she still clung to her juvenile fantasies, imagining herself to be in love with a self-styled genius who probably cared nothing for her.

Pao Tai readily accepted the invitation to dinner, partly for the free meal, but also to meet with Fei again. He should have guessed there was an ulterior motive for the invitation. But he was so entranced by Fei that it never occurred to him to question why he had been invited. Etiquette forbade subjects of importance being broached before the end of the meal, so there was no hint of the letter's existence. It was, at last, raised in conversation after dinner, but so casually, that it came as something of a shock to Pao Tai when he realized he was expected to read it for them.

Pao Tai looked up at Fei, totally smitten by her beauty and innocence. He would never be more than a country boy, yet her heart was set on some rogue who promised her excitement, social position and wealth. The letter in his hand – it could be the key to his own happiness; but what of hers?

'It's a formal notice, and...', he hesitated, '...it is very grave news.'

With a cry, Fei ran from the room. Her mother hurried after her. From the inner room, Pao Tai could hear Fei sobbing, and her mother's soothing voice. Then Fei's mother returned. 'Do not distress yourself, Pao Tai. Perhaps it is for the best. They would never have been happy together.'

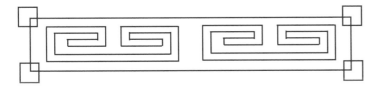

Pao was somewhat surprised when, shortly afterwards, he received another invitation to dine with the family. The atmosphere was cordial, but it seemed to Pao Tai that there was a strange undercurrent of unspoken conspiracy which he could not understand. Then Fei's mother spoke.

'I hope you do not mind, Pao Tai, but when you were unable to read the letter completely, I took it to the astrologer to read. Old Chao told me exactly what the letter said.'

Pao Tai looked up with alarm.

'You were quite right, Pao Tai. It was sent from a dear friend of Hua Lung to my daughter Fei. Knowing that Fei and Hua Lung were so close, it respectfully conveyed the painful news that Hua Lung was no longer in our world.'

Fei's mother gave an understanding smile. 'I expect that my daughter will have to start thinking of a suitable husband soon. Fei was born in the Year of the Dog. And you, I believe, were born in the year of the Horse? Old Chao said that such partners make excellent marriages.'

Fei's grief was short-lived. Her love for Hua Lung was not forgotten, but it now lay in the past. She began to realize that love has many aspects – kindness, consideration, and most of all, the happiness of being loved in return. Somehow, the qualities she had once valued now seemed rather unimportant to her.

One evening, her mother, about to start some sewing, suddenly called out to her. 'Fei, where are my needles? I can't find them anywhere. Can you see them?'

Fei laughed. 'Why, they're right under your nose, pinned to your dress.'

'So they are. "Ride a horse to find a horse", the sages say,' said her mother. 'Often you can't see the thing you want most when it's there, right in front of you.'

Silently, Fei agreed.

Pao Tai and Fei had been happily married for about three years when a most curious incident occurred. Fei happened to be spending a few days away from home with an aunt who had fallen sick. One day, while out shopping in the town, buying a few things for the invalid, she was convinced that she had seen the ghost of Hua Lung. He had even nodded to her.

Puzzled, when returning back home, Fei decided to tackle her husband about something that had bothered her for a long time. Gently, she broached the subject.

'Pao Tai,' she asked, 'That letter you read to my family before we were married. Did it really say that Hua Lung had died?'

Pao Tai looked at his wife and smiled with love and understanding.

'You were so much in love with your dream at the time, I simply couldn't let your illusions about his love for you be shattered in such a devastating way. But no, Hua Lung was alive and well. The letter that had been sent to you was in fact an invitation to his wedding.'

The Dog personality

If you are looking for someone of principle, whose word you can rely on, who would stand by you in times of trouble, and who could be trusted with your most valued possessions or secrets, then you could well be looking for a person born in the year of the Dog.

But although Dog personalities appear to make friends easily, they are naturally defensive and suspicious; and while they tend to have many acquaintances, they form deep attachments with only a few trusted friends. You are lucky indeed if you are accepted as one of the Dog's select company, for you will have a friend for life.

It is natural for the outsider to mistake an easy-going, familiar manner as the invitation to a closer relationship. But it takes a long time for the Dog to forge a working partnership. Unfortunately, this can often lead to serious misunderstandings. The Dog's fiercely defensive temperament may also lead to a breakdown in relationships. A word out of place, or the mere hint of criticism directed at someone or something dear to the Dog's heart, and the Dog can suddenly – sometimes even frighteningly – flare up in a rage. But the anger subsides very quickly, and apologies will be sincere.

With this strong sense of loyalty, it is not particularly surprisingly, therefore, that the typical Dog personality is frequently drawn to joining the uniformed services – defending the country, upholding the law, or caring for the sick, for instance. Regimentation is no hardship to the Dog, who likes and even thrives on order and regularity. But even if a Dog personality does not, literally, wear a uniform, there will still be something of the same air of authority about this zodiac type, whether in the home, at work, or during leisure hours.

In love, the Dog always values a firm and steady relationship – so a life partnership is important. But though that relationship may be strong and enduring, it may not take the form of the singular devotion that might be expected. Indeed, occasional forays beyond the close confines of the committed relationship do not seem to disturb the Dog's conscience unduly. Loyalty, for some Dog personalities, is more loosely interpreted as returning home. The Dog partner may feel guilty for a while, but probably only through fear of the consequences – perhaps threatened break-up of the partnership. A flirtation, the Dog may believe, is only a passing thing. The heart – and that is what matters for the Dog – remains true.

WHO IS THE PERFECT PARTNER FOR THE DOG?

Those who have a Dog personality for a friend are fortunate indeed. Dogs are loyal and faithful companions, and rarely break the bonds of friendship. Consequently, they demand loyalty in return; and those who are not prepared to offer unquestioning allegiance have no place in the Dog's inner circle of friends.

The Dog enjoys the company of those who share the same interests; and being of a practical turn of mind, the Dog usually finds the ambitious Tiger or the hard-working Horse ideal companions. But the Dog can also be dazzled by the more exotic and exuberant characters of the Chinese zodiac. The Dragon's magnetism and charm, for example, will be dangerously fascinating; the Snake's mysterious sensuality will hypnotize; and the flamboyant extravagance of the Rooster, astonish. Nevertheless, the Dog is often reluctant to commit himself or herself to any of these colourful personalities. Dog-types have enough common sense to realize that, exciting as these people are, there is likely to be little common ground between them.

Conversely, the Dog has no time for solidly reliable types like the Ox or the Sheep; they do not have the Dog's ability to make sudden decisions and act on the whim of the moment. When it comes to choosing a life partner, therefore, the Dog would do well to take the line of least resistance and settle down with the person next door – astrologically speaking. For the Dog's complementary sign is the comfort-loving Pig (next in the zodiac listing), who will be only too happy to provide all the Dog's material needs. Perhaps it is not so remarkable that it should be the easy-going and carefree Pig who best understands the reasons for the Dog's changes of mood and temperament.

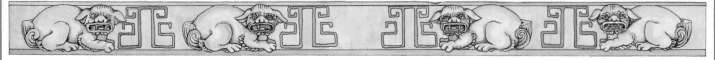

How each of the twelve personality types ————— relates to the Dog —————

With THE RAT
Although dogs and rats are enemies in the natural world, astrologically they can become firm and loyal companions. But each partner needs to be aware of the other's negative side. The Rat should beware the Dog's short fuse, and be prepared for occasional bouts of irrational anger; the Dog must accept that the Rat's personality is a complex one. Both the Rat and the Dog come to life at night, but while the Dog wants to play, the Rat may put its mind to more serious matters. If, by chance, passion dies, and the relationship ends, they will nevertheless stay in touch, delighted to exchange news about each other's progress in life.

With THE OX
There must be something special in a relationship that binds the Ox and Dog together, for they seem to have little in common. Their interests, attitudes and outlooks on life are so contrasting that it seems all they could ever do is argue. But, in most cases when two people are astrologically incompatible, the presence of a third person in the family often acts as a balancing factor. For example, a child born in the year of the Rat would restore harmony to this troubled couple. Even lovemaking is likely to be tempestuous; indeed, they are rarely able to agree what it is that they want from the relationship unless firm guidelines are set.

With THE TIGER
The Tiger makes one of the best partners for the Dog personality. They share many interests, and both are able to add that little extra to make the relationship special. Each admires the other's qualities and skills, secretly flattered to be so genuinely appreciated. Although both partners are used to taking the lead, there is a more-than-usual willingness to give and take. Such harmony is reflected in their love-life, too. Eager to please the other, either partner will lead, follow, experiment or continue the well-trodden path.

With THE HARE
For the Dog, the Hare is far from ideal. Although the Hare has many of the characteristics of its companion sign, the Tiger – one of the best matches for the Dog – these shared qualities are not the ones that fulfil the Dog's needs. Although the Dog will find the Hare responsive and willing, and the Hare will discover the Dog to be honest and dependable, the Dog may make unfair comparisons with other couples, and yearn for something more stimulating. Perhaps the Hare's compliance is the root of the problem. Independence of spirit, spontaneity and sparkle may be what is needed to keep this relationship alive.

With THE DRAGON
Here is a magical personality who can dazzle the Dog. Full of admiration for the Dragon's ways with words, its handling of people, and sheer effrontery, the Dog often falls completely under the Dragon's spell. But the attraction does not last forever. When it comes to practicalities, the Dog will realize that the heady pleasures of life with the Dragon are all too shallow; and the sooner the two come to terms with real life, the better. In love and romance, however, even if the partnership breaks down, the Dragon will have opened a new world of experience for the Dog.

With THE SNAKE
In this relationship, the Dog is drawn by the Snake's sensuality, readily falling for its charms. But this is not an ideal partnership, being founded on physical attraction alone, rather than spiritual kinship. However, it may last longer than expected. The Snake is alert to the Dog's feelings, though the Dog may come to believe that the Snake's feelings can never be truly fathomed. This can make the Dog feel emotionally inferior. But if the couple have a child, particularly one born in a Rooster year, balance and harmony can be restored to make the relationship a lasting success.

With THE HORSE

Few partnerships are more successful than that of the Dog and Horse personalities. They have many shared interests, and probably see something of themselves in the partner. However, oddly enough, they would never describe themselves as being devoted to each other – indeed, they might be remarkably surprised to be told that they are in love. For these two types, the relationship is such a natural extension of friendship that love may have developed unnoticed. As for physical love between these two, there is no shortage. Their outlook on life is one of frank openness; there are no moral or religious taboos, and they are not at all afraid to discuss matters sexual, either in private or with anyone who is prepared to listen.

With THE SHEEP

There is something about the Sheep personality that sets the Dog's teeth on edge. It may be the Sheep's opposite outlook on life, fashion sense or even physical appearance, which are contrary to the Dog's imagined ideal partner. So when Dog and Sheep get together, something must be at work which is more powerful than mere physical attraction. This being the case, the two can form a lasting partnership which will outlive passion and romance. A loving relationship may result, but it is unlikely to be of the conventional sort.

With THE MONKEY

This is one of those relationships that is a mystery to outsiders. The Monkey and Dog seem to have little in common – their interests may differ widely and there may be a great difference in age – yet each has a special understanding of the other's needs. They share many secrets, perhaps even having a private language of their own, while their sense of humour can be baffling to others. It is difficult to penetrate their closeness; and initially, at least, this frequently causes anxiety among friends or relatives who may well feel left out and forgotten. As parents, the Dog and the Monkey are likely to be quite unconventional, and have radical ideas on the best ways to bring up children – ideas that they might find raises opposition among those who believe they know better.

With THE ROOSTER

Too close for comfort – that just about sums up the frequent tension between the Dog and Rooster personalities that may arise if they form a permanent relationship. It is likely that these two animal types met through being neighbours, studying at school together, or working in the same office. And although they may be close in many ways, even physically, there is an invisible divide that separates the Dog from the Rooster. They will never fully understand each other, no matter how deep their feelings are. There is a tendency for both partners to go their own separate ways on occasions, but they rarely divulge what they have been doing. And the partner is wise not to ask. This is a relationship that requires constant compromise, but if the two have learnt how to cope in this way, the relationship may well last and lead to a happy coexistence.

With ANOTHER DOG

Most personalities who share the same sign get on well together. In romance, Dog-types have similar interests, the same outlook on life, and the same determination to make life interesting – even exciting. Yet, without outside stimulus, something may seem to be lacking, and there is a danger that this relationship could go stale before too long if this is not realized. However, Dog partners are likely to stay together for so long that they would be past caring anyway by the time they eventually found out what it was they had needed to strengthen their relationship.

With THE PIG

For a Dog who desires to set up a comfortable home, and raise a family of happy children, the Pig is an ideal partner – even more so if the Dog is the male and the Pig, the female. Each is able to offer the other a closeness born of inner understanding. Though the Pig may seem a little unadventurous for the Dog at times, and though the Dog may stray away from the hearth just occasionally but not wholeheartedly, theirs is a love that can overcome any such temporary breaks. They may even find that, by giving each other a little room, the partnership benefits in the long run.

CHAPTER TWELVE
THE PIG

Building a new stove

Mr Chu patted the arm of his favourite chair.

'Well, old friend, we've seen life out together so far, but I think we'll be parting company soon.'

'All good things have to come to an end,' his wife said consolingly, bringing him green tea. She tucked the blanket around his shoulders a little more firmly to make him more comfortable.

'When the wedding is over, and the last of our children has gone, we'll be happier in a smaller house,' she said unconvincingly. 'As it is, we have too many things that are of no use to us.'

'I know,' he replied, with resignation. 'Still, they all bring back memories. But our dear Mei-li is going to have a proper wedding. I spoke to old Tsan about selling some of our little treasures.'

'What about this for a start?,' said his wife, delicately handing him a prized piece of porcelain. 'I never did like this plate with all those snakes on it.'

Mr Chu laughed. 'If anything has to go from this house, that would have to go first. Snakes have no place in a house full of Pigs, as our astrologer friend has told us so often.'

Mrs Chu smiled. 'The Snake bowl it is, then. I'll put it in a box for you to take to Old Tsan the next time you go out. But don't take his first offer, mind. You know what a tricky one he is. Every copper coin has to be counted at the time. Get twenty strings of cash at least, and our friends will have plenty of wine. Get fifty, and we can have a real feast.'

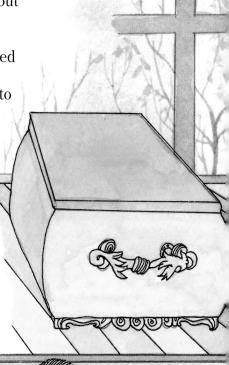

Mei-li, their daughter, smiled, adding: 'And if you can get a hundred, Father, I might get a beautiful wedding dress, too!' Her father, took her hands gently. 'My lovely girl, you will have a wedding dress even if it means the guests have to drink rice-water.'

In truth, Mr Chu was very worried about their financial state. The little income he had would no longer suffice to keep them both in retirement; and although they had saved to cover the expenses of getting Mei-li married, the costs had been much more than he expected. Selling the home, which had been in his family for generations, was the only solution.

But there were even more pressing things to consider. Mr Chu had already received visits from the marriage-broker, who brought red cards from interested parties. The first had come from a certain Mr Hui. He was a wealthy landowner, and Mr Chu would have had no financial problems if he had accepted the proposal. But Mr Hui proved to be a widower older than himself, and Mr Chu – despite the prospect of his daughter marrying into riches – could not face the idea of his son-in-law being senior in age.

Mr Chu, therefore, consulted an astrologer to dispel his doubts. It was pointed out that Mr Hui had been born in the year of the Monkey. And since Mei-li, like both her parents, was born in the year of the Pig, she and Mr Hui were incompatible. This, of course, gave Mr Chu a suitably diplomatic excuse for refusing the offer.

A second visit from the marriage-broker brought a red card from the parents of Tan Ho, a handsome young man born in the year of the Sheep. Mr Chu very discreetly checked up on the family's credentials, and was delighted to discover not only that Sheep and Pig were compatible, but also that the suitor met with Mei-li's approval. He thus sent a red card back to the young man's parents, indicating that Tan Ho would be an acceptable son-in-law.

Now there came the exchange of presents. To Mr Chu's alarm, the presents sent by Tan Ho's parents – some beautiful sandalwood furniture for the future home – proved to be much more lavish than expected. He dared not be shamed into offering inferior gifts, and decided to call on Mr Tsan. Although the latter styled himself an antiquarian dealer, Mr Tsan was in effect a pawnbroker.

He examined the snake-encrusted bowl with great interest. 'Yes,' he said, 'pieces like this certainly look valuable, although there is no great demand for such ornate decoration. But I would like to help you with your daughter's wedding. If you are agreeable, I could advance you a loan against it – shall we say a hundred strings of cash?'
Mr Chu gasped. 'A hundred?'
Old Mr Tsan shrugged his shoulders. 'Very well, a hundred and fifty. But that's my final offer.'
Mr Chu nodded in agreement, trying to conceal his excitement. His daughter would have a splendid wedding dress, and there would be meat, fish and wine on the tables to offer their guests after all.

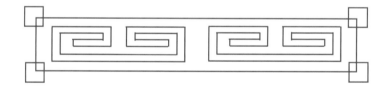

On the day of Mei-li's wedding, the winter sky was clear and blue, with just a few flecks of snow dazzling on the ground. Through the crisp, cool air came the clanging of cymbals and drums, as a little procession made its way to the Chu's house.

Mei-li was dressed as finely as any Chinese girl could hope to be on her wedding day. The scarlet robe, embroidered with dragons and phoenixes, was decorated with pearls and gold thread, and she wore a tinkling head-dress which glittered with florets of beaten gold and deep red coral.

With her heart pounding, Mei-li was lifted into a sedan-chair. She could be forgiven for looking tense and serious, since the least movement tended to spoil the effect of her elegant dress. The whole household now followed the chair through the town to the house of Tan Ho's family. Mei-li stepped down and, with her new husband, went into the reception room where a family altar had been placed. Together with Tan Ho, Mei-li pledged her homage to his ancestors, signifying that she now abandoned all ties with her family. Mrs Chu blinked and gripped her husband's arm.

Once the official part of the ceremony was over, Tan Ho's father called on everyone to join in the feasting and celebrations. There was wine to be drunk, speeches to be said, and many people to meet.

Much to Mr Chu's irritation, however, he was accosted by Old Tsan, the antiquarian dealer. Poking him in the ribs, Tsan said: 'I have some good news for you, Mr Chu. I have managed to find a purchaser. With your permission, I will write off the debt.' But Mr Chu was too distracted by the guests to attend to business. 'That seems a good idea,' he replied, and went off to join the wedding party.

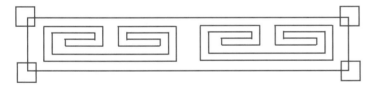

Much later, the Chu's returned home. 'We might as well enjoy our last few moments here,' said Mr Chu philosophically.
'Hush dear,' replied his wife. 'Once we have sold the house, we will have enough to live comfortably for the rest of our days. Cheer up!'

Suddenly, a carriage, decorated with a nobleman's flag, drew up to the house, and a distinguished-looking gentleman, who was attended by several servants, got out and approached them.

'My dear Mr Chu,' replied the stranger, 'I have come to thank you for your remarkable discovery. It has taken me some time to find you. Your friend Mr Tsan was for some reason most reluctant to tell me where you lived. Curiosity forces me to ask you where you obtained the Snake bowl.'
'The one I sold to Mr Tsan? It was part of an old family heirloom, passed down from my grandfather. I remember that he had won it for some heroic act,' replied Mr Chu, wondering why the stranger should wish to know this.

The nobleman then explained: 'The bowl you sold to Mr Tsan is one of a set of twelve which were commissioned by the rebel Yuan Emperor as a birthday gift for his Empress. Each bowl, representing one of the twelve animals of the zodiac, was painted by a different artist, the twelve most famous of their day. The sixth, your Snake bowl, was created by none other than the Master Yu Ti.

'But when the rebel Emperor was overthrown by loyal troops, the palace and virtually everything in it were destroyed – except, apparently, the Snake bowl which came into your possession.

'The loss of the other eleven is certainly a tragedy, but the fact that you have managed to preserve this one remaining masterpiece is a marvel. It is therefore my great privilege to tell you that the Emperor has commanded that the Snake bowl should be placed in the Imperial Treasury, and in future it will be known as the Bowl of Palace Guardian Mr Chu. I hope the two thousand which I gave your friend as payment for the Snake bowl was sufficient for you?'

Mrs Chu sat down, a strange expression on her face. Then, silently, she got up, walked across the room, and opened a chest. From it, she took out another bowl decorated with little pigs, and carefully handed it to the distinguished visitor. 'Would the Emperor perhaps be interested in the rest of the set?' she asked him.

The Pig personality

Understandably, some in the West may not find it at all flattering to discover that their Chinese birth sign is the Pig. But, in fact, of all the signs of the Chinese zodiac, this is the happiest. Indeed, those who are fortunate enough to be born under this sign may not be destined to enjoy riches and power, but they will delight in the far more valuable gifts of contentment, comfort and satisfaction. Pig personalities are considerate and compassionate people who are never short of sympathy or affection. And since they care so much for others, they will ensure that their home is always a welcome haven for family, friends, and those in need.

Pig personalities are extremely industrious, too, for they know that peace and security are not achieved easily, and that leisure and pleasure are the rewards of determination. It is a great pity, however, that being so kind-hearted is sometimes a failing, for it is only too easy for the unscrupulous to take advantage of the Pig.

As a measure of the high esteem in which the Chinese hold the Pig, the Chinese character for 'home' actually represents a roof with a Pig underneath it – symbolizing the association between homeliness and this animal sign.

Like its companion sign, the Dog, the Pig is concerned with home life; but whereas the Dog is preoccupied with the actual structure of the house – making it safe against the weather and intruders – the Pig is more concerned about making it a place of contentment. While the Dog ensures that the roof does not leak, the Pig makes sure that the hearth is always as welcoming as possible.

Pig personalities are extremely sociable by nature, and will have a wide variety of friends. But rather than visiting night-spots, they prefer t o entertain at home. Indeed, both male and female Pig-types have excellent domestic skills, and make superb cooks. Despite their appreciation of good cuisine, however, they are not inclined to take up catering professionally. Instead, Pig-types are more likely to be drawn to careers that centre on welfare, such as the education of the young, child-care, looking after the elderly or nursing.

But if the Pig's inclination is more towards business than a profession, then soft furnishings, kitchen equipment, interior decoration and all matters to do with transforming a house into a home will be profitable areas of employment.

WHO IS THE PERFECT PARTNER FOR THE PIG?

A Pig transforms a house into a home. But while Pig people may be valuable partners for anyone wanting to settle down and raise a family, they make poor travelling companions for those set on a life of adventure, being constantly anxious about what may be happening back home.

As for Pig personalities themselves, they will not relish providing a home for someone who is hardly ever there, nor for some wastrel who is going to squander the housekeeping. The Pig needs someone to share and appreciate the comforts that a home can provide, and who will help to make that home a desirable place in which to be. Love is one thing, and common sense another. But the Pig personality is often not a good judge of character. Take the Snake and the Dragon, for example. The Snake may well exude a certain hypnotic charm, and the Dragon astonish by its successful life-style. But these are not really the kinds of people with whom Pig personalities should spend the rest of their lives. Nor should the Pig get too interested in the Tiger or the Monkey. The Tiger is much too authoritarian and restrictive to allow the Pig any freedom; while conversely, the fickle Monkey is often far too unreliable.

Provided that a happy family life is the first consideration, and career prospects are not uppermost in the Pig's mind, the ideal companion will be another Pig. For more excitement, but shared understanding, the Dog follows closely. Those Pigs who would dearly love a large family should choose a Sheep or a Hare for their life's companion; while for the professional or business-minded Pig, looking for a partner who can bring fresh ideas to the partnership, the Pig could consider the reliable Ox or the stimulating Rooster.

How each of the twelve personality types relates to the Pig

With THE RAT

These two people seem so different in every way, that outsiders might wonder how they ever came to be friends, let alone lovers. And yet there is nothing really remarkable about their relationship – they are merely two contented people, happy with each other's company. Like most couples, they have their disputes and misunderstandings, but these are usually over trivialities which do not affect the essential stability of the partnership. Each gets on with life quite happily, and is pleased that the partner does not interfere too greatly in aspects of life that they are not inclined to share. Their love-life is fresh and unpredictable.

With THE OX

For the Pig who sometimes needs the support and encouragement of a stronger-minded partner, the Ox is the ideal companion. Whether this takes the form of financial help, practical assistance or a psychological boost now and then, the Ox can be relied upon to provide it. In return, the Pig will provide all the love, affection and devotion that the Ox needs. A sound family circle is essential to the welfare of both these types, and each is able to contribute in its own way. Though some may think they lead dull and routine lives, this is the way they prefer things.

With THE TIGER

It is easy to see why the Pig is attracted to the charismatic Tiger, but less easy to appreciate how this couple – with all their differences – manage to stay together for long. The Tiger may mix with exciting and stimulating company, yet yearn for the quietness and calm that the Pig – an exceptional homemaker – can provide. To ensure that the partnership survives, the Tiger partner must take care that the Pig is not overwhelmed by the Tiger's insistence on taking the initiative all the time; and the Pig will need properly to appreciate the Tiger's need for outside interests.

With THE HARE

With a Hare for a partner, the Pig personality has a rewarding life ahead, for this relationship is one of the most successful and contented that the Pig could hope for. This couple can expect to have their house full of happy, healthy children – and, in the years to come, numerous grandchildren, too. This is a loving partnership, in which the physical side of the relationship is rich and satisfying. The home life of Hare and Pig will be the envy of couples whose lives are less happily organized, and they are likely to have a constant stream of visitors who enjoy the contented atmosphere they create.

With THE DRAGON

There is generally something less than fulfilling about this partnership – perhaps it is the noticeable age difference or the fact that the couple could well be from different social backgrounds. So, as close as this couple may be to each other in their love-life, there are always hidden depths that can never be fully shared. It is a pity that the Dragon leans so heavily on the Pig's shoulders, for there are times when the Pig is desperate for encouragement and support, and the Dragon should provide this. By the same token, it would do no harm if the Dragon were to be more demonstrative in its affection towards the Pig partner.

With THE SNAKE

This may not be the most satisfying of relationships. Indeed, if they start to find that they treat each other as rivals, one always trying to score points off the other's failures, it will be time for a serious talk. Life may be a game, but when two people decide to embark on a relationship, they ought to be on the same side. Soon, the time may come to discuss precisely what each is hoping to gain from the partnership. Snake and Pig need to learn to give, as well as take, in order for the relationship to succeed.

With THE HORSE
These two types are so self-sufficient that it is hard to think of them being involved in a relationship at all. Nevertheless, there is a great deal of affection in the partnership, and the physical side of their love cannot be faulted. They have every confidence in themselves and each other, and are frank and open about their needs and feelings. If anything at all is lacking, it may be a sense of mystery or surprise so that the initial spark can remain kindled. They should try to introduce a touch of excitement and romance into their lives, and avoid being too predictable, for any sign of stale routine will come to be resented and possibly weaken the partnership.

With THE SHEEP
This is an idyllic relationship. Indeed, they will be as contented as the happy Pig and Hare couple, though perhaps not as boisterous. For Sheep are ideal partners for those Pig personalities who prefer a quiet life, like to get everything organized, and look forward to having a warm and loving family around them with the minimum of trouble and fuss. The Sheep will be quite happy to leave everything in the Pig's capable hands, and will be a supportive partner when encouragement is needed. Their love for each other encompasses all their emotional and physical needs. There is tenderness, romance, passion and affection in this relationship; and they will find joy in their children who will surely benefit from having such a stable family background.

With THE MONKEY
Despite the fact that the Pig and the Monkey are well-loved characters in Chinese fiction, they are traditional enemies. Indeed, an old Chinese proverb states that when the Pig meets the Monkey, there are always tears. Chinese astrologers, too, shake their heads at this relationship, and would not advise it. So, if these two are determined to stick together, they must be prepared to make allowances for each other's personal foibles, and at the same time do their utmost to show each other the greatest care and consideration. The key word here will be compromise.

With THE ROOSTER
Though they are not the ideal couple, there is great advantage to be gained from such a partnership. Both will see new aspects to life, and be richer for the experience. This relationship will work most effectively if the Rooster is the male partner, for a male Pig partner may find the Rooster rather a wearisome companion at times. The romantic side of their relationship may be quiet and low-key, but they will both make a special effort to remember birthdays, anniversaries and other special occasions, which they will celebrate in style. Nevertheless, they may feel that something is lacking in their lives – perhaps in connection with their lovemaking. They must learn to share their feelings, otherwise the partnership could begin to drift apart.

With THE DOG
This is an ideal relationship for two young people wanting to set up together in life, and facing an uncertain future. But they must not expect life to run too smoothly, for they both have to work, in their own characteristic ways, at building a life together. The Dog's special gifts will be put to good use in making a sound and secure home for the family to live in; while the caring Pig will tend and cherish the family. The attraction between them is both emotionally rich and physically fulfilling. No matter what obstacles may stand in the way, their affection and need for each other will be enduring.

With ANOTHER PIG
As a rule, people with the same zodiacal sign are compatible, and there is no truer example of this than a happy Pig couple. Not only is their affection for each other extremely strong, but their happiness is infectious, bringing love and laughter to all those fortunate enough to be near to them. They may never be rich, for they are far too generous for their own good; but their children will never be in want, since – in their parents' eyes – the offsprings' needs are always a priority. Whatever Pig personalities look for in a relationship – whether it is romance, companionship or passion – a Pig partner can provide it.

GENERAL TABLE OF ANIMAL YEARS

You can use this General Table to find your animal sign only if your birthdate falls after February 20th or before January 20th. Please note, however, that if the latter is the case, your animal sign will be the one belonging to the previous year. If your birthdate falls between January 20th and February 20th, you should consult the Special Table of Animal Years on page 109.

RAT	1900	1912	1924	1936	1948	1960	1972	1984	1996	2008	2020
OX	1901	1913	1925	1937	1949	1961	1973	1985	1997	2009	2021
TIGER	1902	1914	1926	1938	1950	1962	1974	1986	1998	2010	2022
HARE	1903	1915	1927	1939	1951	1963	1975	1987	1999	2011	2023
DRAGON	1904	1916	1928	1940	1952	1964	1976	1988	2000	2012	2024
SNAKE	1905	1917	1929	1941	1953	1965	1977	1989	2001	2013	2025
HORSE	1906	1918	1930	1942	1954	1966	1978	1990	2002	2014	2026
SHEEP	1907	1919	1931	1943	1955	1967	1979	1991	2003	2015	2027
MONKEY	1908	1920	1932	1944	1956	1968	1980	1992	2004	2016	2028
ROOSTER	1909	1921	1933	1945	1957	1969	1981	1993	2005	2017	2029
DOG	1910	1922	1934	1946	1958	1970	1982	1994	2006	2018	2030
PIG	1911	1923	1935	1947	1959	1971	1983	1995	2007	2019	2031

SPECIAL TABLE OF ANIMAL YEARS

The date of the Chinese New Year is different each year, and may be as late as February 20th. If your birthday falls *after* February 20th, you can find your Chinese zodiac sign at a glance by looking for your year of birth in the last column of the table. Your Chinese zodiac sign is shown next to it. If, however, your birthday occurs before February 20th, your sign may be the previous year's. In this case, check the table in the following way.

First find your year of birth in the last column, then look at the date of the Chinese New Year for that particular year.

If your birthday fell *before* the Chinese New Year that year, your zodiac sign is the one in the first column. Otherwise, your sign is the one next to your year of birth. The table continues on the next page.

If your birthday fell before the Chinese New Year	Chinese New Year	If your birthday fell on or after the Chinese New Year	
RAT	Feb 19	OX	1901
OX	Feb 8	TIGER	1902
TIGER	Jan 29	HARE	1903
HARE	Feb 16	DRAGON	1904
DRAGON	Feb 4	SNAKE	1905
SNAKE	Jan 25	HORSE	1906
HORSE	Feb 13	SHEEP	1907
SHEEP	Feb 2	MONKEY	1908
MONKEY	Jan 22	ROOSTER	1909
ROOSTER	Feb 10	DOG	1910
DOG	Jan 30	PIG	1911
PIG	Feb 18	RAT	1912
RAT	Feb 6	OX	1913
OX	Jan 26	TIGER	1914
TIGER	Feb 14	HARE	1915
HARE	Feb 3	DRAGON	1916
DRAGON	Jan 23	SNAKE	1917
SNAKE	Feb 11	HORSE	1918
HORSE	Feb 1	SHEEP	1919
SHEEP	Feb 20	MONKEY	1920
MONKEY	Feb 8	ROOSTER	1921
ROOSTER	Jan 28	DOG	1922

If your birthday fell before the Chinese New Year	Chinese New Year	If your birthday fell on or after the Chinese New Year	
DOG	Feb 16	PIG	1923
PIG	Feb 5	RAT	1924
RAT	Jan 25	OX	1925
OX	Feb 13	TIGER	1926
TIGER	Feb 2	HARE	1927
HARE	Jan 23	DRAGON	1928
DRAGON	Feb 10	SNAKE	1929
SNAKE	Jan 30	HORSE	1930
HORSE	Feb 17	SHEEP	1931
SHEEP	Feb 6	MONKEY	1932
MONKEY	Jan 26	ROOSTER	1933
ROOSTER	Feb 14	DOG	1934
DOG	Feb 4	PIG	1935
PIG	Jan 24	RAT	1936
RAT	Feb 11	OX	1937
OX	Jan 31	TIGER	1938
TIGER	Feb 19	HARE	1939
HARE	Feb 8	DRAGON	1940
DRAGON	Jan 27	SNAKE	1941
SNAKE	Feb 15	HORSE	1942
HORSE	Feb 5	SHEEP	1943
SHEEP	Jan 25	MONKEY	1944
MONKEY	Feb 13	ROOSTER	1945
ROOSTER	Feb 2	DOG	1946
DOG	Jan 22	PIG	1947
PIG	Feb 10	RAT	1948
RAT	Jan 29	OX	1949
OX	Feb 17	TIGER	1950
TIGER	Feb 6	HARE	1951
HARE	Jan 27	DRAGON	1952
DRAGON	Feb 14	SNAKE	1953
SNAKE	Feb 3	HORSE	1954
HORSE	Jan 24	SHEEP	1955
SHEEP	Feb 12	MONKEY	1956
MONKEY	Jan 31	ROOSTER	1957
ROOSTER	Feb 18	DOG	1958
DOG	Feb 8	PIG	1959
PIG	Jan 28	RAT	1960

If your birthday fell before the Chinese New Year	Chinese New Year	If your birthday fell on or after the Chinese New Year	
RAT	Feb 15	OX	1961
OX	Feb 5	TIGER	1962
TIGER	Jan 25	HARE	1963
HARE	Feb 13	DRAGON	1964
DRAGON	Feb 2	SNAKE	1965
SNAKE	Jan 21	HORSE	1966
HORSE	Feb 9	SHEEP	1967
SHEEP	Jan 30	MONKEY	1968
MONKEY	Feb 17	ROOSTER	1969
ROOSTER	Feb 6	DOG	1970
DOG	Jan 27	PIG	1971
PIG	Feb 15	RAT	1972
RAT	Feb 3	OX	1973
OX	Jan 23	TIGER	1974
TIGER	Feb 11	HARE	1975
HARE	Jan 31	DRAGON	1976
DRAGON	Feb 18	SNAKE	1977
SNAKE	Feb 7	HORSE	1978
HORSE	Jan 28	SHEEP	1979
SHEEP	Feb 16	MONKEY	1980
MONKEY	Feb 5	ROOSTER	1981
ROOSTER	Jan 25	DOG	1982
DOG	Feb 13	PIG	1983
PIG	Feb 2	RAT	1984
RAT	Feb 20	OX	1985
OX	Feb 9	TIGER	1986
TIGER	Jan 29	HARE	1987
HARE	Feb 17	DRAGON	1988
DRAGON	Feb 6	SNAKE	1989
SNAKE	Jan 27	HORSE	1990
HORSE	Feb 15	SHEEP	1991
SHEEP	Feb 4	MONKEY	1992
MONKEY	Jan 23	ROOSTER	1993
ROOSTER	Feb 10	DOG	1994
DOG	Jan 31	PIG	1995
PIG	Feb 19	RAT	1996
RAT	Feb 7	OX	1997
OX	Jan 28	TIGER	1998

If your birthday fell before the Chinese New Year	Chinese New Year	If your birthday fell on or after the Chinese New Year	
TIGER	Feb 16	HARE	1999
HARE	Feb 5	DRAGON	2000
DRAGON	Jan 24	SNAKE	2001
SNAKE	Feb 12	HORSE	2002
HORSE	Feb 1	SHEEP	2003
SHEEP	Jan 22	MONKEY	2004
MONKEY	Feb 9	ROOSTER	2005
ROOOSTER	Jan 29	DOG	2006
DOG	Feb 18	PIG	2007
PIG	Feb 7	RAT	2008
RAT	Jan 26	OX	2009
OX	Feb 14	TIGER	2010
TIGER	Feb 3	HARE	2011
HARE	Jan 23	DRAGON	2012
DRAGON	Feb 10	SNAKE	2013
SNAKE	Jan 31	HORSE	2014
HORSE	Feb 19	SHEEP	2015
SHEEP	Feb 8	MONKEY	2016
MONKEY	Jan 28	ROOSTER	2017
ROOSTER	Feb 16	DOG	2018
DOG	Feb 5	PIG	2019
PIG	Jan 25	RAT	2020
RAT	Feb 12	OX	2021
OX	Feb 1	TIGER	2022
TIGER	Jan 22	HARE	2023
HARE	Feb 10	DRAGON	2024
DRAGON	Jan 29	SNAKE	2025

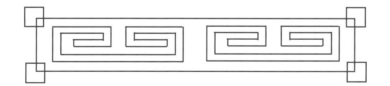